D0594193

ALSO BY AL RIES AND LAURA RIES

The Origin of Brands
The Fall of Advertising & the Rise of PR
The 11 Immutable Laws of Internet Branding
The 22 Immutable Laws of Branding

ALSO BY AL RIES

Focus: The Future of Your Company Depends on It
The 22 Immutable Laws of Marketing*
Horse Sense*
Bottom-up Marketing*
Marketing Warfare*
Positioning: The Battle for Your Mind*

*with Jack Trout

WAR IN THE BOARD ROOM

Why Left-Brain Management and Right-Brain Marketing Don't See Eye-to-Eye— and What to Do About It

AL & LAURA RIES

COLLINS BUSINESS
An Imprint of HarperCollinsPublishers

WAR IN THE BOARDROOM. Copyright © 2009 by Al and Laura Ries. All rights reserved. Printed in the United States of America. No part of this book may be used or reproduced in any manner whatsoever without written permission except in the case of brief quotations embodied in critical articles and reviews. For information, address HarperCollins Publishers, 10 East 53rd Street, New York, NY 10022.

HarperCollins books may be purchased for educational, business, or sales promotional use. For information, please write: Special Markets Department, HarperCollins Publishers, 10 East 53rd Street, New York, NY 10022.

FIRST EDITION

Designed by Renato Stanisic

Library of Congress Cataloging-in-Publication Data
   Ries, Al.
      War in the boardroom : why left-brain management and right-brain marketing don't see eye-to-eye—and what to do about it / Al & Laura Ries.
         p.   cm.
      Includes index.
      ISBN 978-0-06-166919-4
      1. Marketing—Psychological aspects. 2. Management—Psychological aspects. 3. Left and right (Psychology) 4. Organizational effectiveness. 5. Success in business. I. Ries, Laura. II. Title. III. Title: Left-brain management and right-brain marketing. IV. Title: Right-brain marketing.
   HF5415.R443 2009
   658—dc22   2008038182

09 10 11 12 13 OV/RRD 10 9 8 7 6 5 4 3 2 1

ACC LIBRARY SERVICES
AUSTIN, TX

DEDICATED TO
peace in the boardroom

Contents

CONTENTS

CONTENTS

Contents

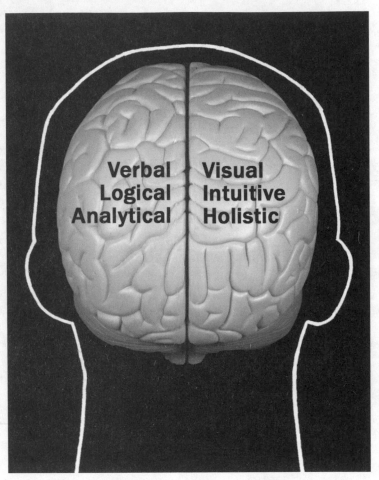

Management tends to attract left brainers,
people who are verbal, logical, and analytical.
Marketing tends to attract right brainers,
people who are visual, intuitive, and holistic.

Preface: Your Divided Brain

Your brain is divided into two completely separate hemispheres. Each hemisphere processes information differently.

Your left hemisphere processes information in series. It thinks in language. It works linearly and methodically.

Your right hemisphere processes information in parallel. It thinks in mental images. It "sees" the big picture.

One side of your brain or the other is dominant. In itself, that should not be surprising since it's consistent with another well-known human trait.

Some people are left-handed and some people are right-handed. In a similar fashion, some people are left brainers and some people are right brainers.

(The two are independent. Left brainers can be either right-handed or left-handed. And vice versa.)

What are you?

If you're the CEO of a major corporation, chances are good you are a left brainer. Before you make a decision, you want to be supported by facts, figures, market data, consumer research. It couldn't be otherwise in a world where the ultimate measurement is the bottom line and the stock price.

If you have a job in marketing, chances are good you are a right brainer. You often make decisions by "gut instinct" with little or no supporting evidence. It couldn't be otherwise in a creative discipline like marketing.

Verbal vs. visual thinking.

Another striking difference: left brainers have a strong preference for verbal thinking, while right brainers favor visual thinking.

When a management type makes a speech, he or she usually stands behind a podium and reads a script or the words on a teleprompter.

When a marketing type makes a speech, he or she usually stands in front of a screen using dozens of visuals.

Even when a left brainer uses PowerPoint slides, the visuals usually aren't visuals. They're usually nothing but words.

Because they are verbally oriented, left-brain people are usually good talkers. Right-brain people are usually good writers.

Why are right brainers good writers? Because arranging words on a page is as much a visual challenge as it is a verbal one. In letters and e-mails, for example, right brainers will often arrange the words so that each line contains a complete thought.

Analytic vs. holistic thinking.

Then there are the left brainers who developed the art and science of risk management. They hired PhDs to build sophisticated computer systems to comb through complicated mortgage portfolios to analyze everything that could possibly go wrong.

Now it looks as if they missed about $700 billion worth of things that could possibly go wrong.

Right-brain holistic thinkers would have looked at the big picture. Why are they lending money to people who can't afford to pay it back?

The computer is the ultimate left-brain machine—magnificent at analyzing and keeping track of millions of details, but totally lost when it comes to looking for the big picture.

Wall Street's reliance on computers to determine investment risks is typical left-brain lunacy. As Warren Buffett once said, "Beware of geeks bearing formulas."

An electronic brain can only look backwards; it can only analyze existing data. A human brain, especially one with a right-brain bias, can "visualize" what might happen in the future.

Certainty vs. uncertainty.

Logical, analytical thinking tends to build confidence in a person's ability to predict the future. After all, if you've studied a situation in great detail, then you should be able to foresee what will happen next.

That's why left-brain leaders often have supreme confidence in their ability to do just that.

If there are a number of strategic moves on the table, there's no room for discussion if a CEO weighs in with his or her assessment of the future. "We will do strategic move A because it will produce the best results over the foreseeable future." Discussion over.

We have left meetings like this totally frustrated. There's no point arguing with a CEO who has an uncanny ability to know exactly what is going to happen should a company adopt a particular strategy.

Did you know, for example, that all printed media, including the book you are reading, are going to be obsolete by 2017? At least that's what Microsoft CEO Steve Ballmer predicted back in 2007.

"Within 10 years, the consumption of anything we think of as media today, whether it is print, TV, or the Internet will in fact be delivered over IP and will be digital," said Mr. Ballmer. "Everything will be delivered digitally. Everything you read, you'll read on a screen."

As we remember, radio was going to make newspapers and magazines obsolete. Television was going to make radio obsolete. And the Internet was going to make everything obsolete. We'll see.

"Certainty" is the mark of a left brainer, whereas holistic right brainers are never quite sure. (The world is too big, too complicated, and too confusing for any one person to comprehend.)

If you are uncertain of the outcome of a number of different strategies, then you are more likely to take a chance on a novel concept.

Once again, what are you?

While it would be nice to think you could operate both sides of your brain with equal facility, the research suggests otherwise.

Ambidexterity vs. ambibrainerity.

Take ambidexterity, a condition that is extremely rare. Most people who are thought to be ambidextrous (switchhitters in baseball, for example) are really left-handers who, with a great deal of practice, have taught themselves right-handed skills. Or vice versa.

Ambibrainerity is also extremely rare. While you can learn to exercise the less-favored half of your brain, working both sides equally is almost impossible. Depending on how you were born, you are going to have to live your life either as a left brainer or a right brainer.

That's not necessarily bad.

It takes all types to make the world go round. It takes artists and bankers. Accountants and musicians. Schoolteachers and real-estate agents. Writers and engineers. Architects and lawyers.

Every occupation seems to attract people who favor one side of their brain or the other. It might take logical, analytical thinking to run a corporation, but it also takes intuitive, holistic thinking to run the marketing program for that same corporation.

Once more, what are you?

When first exposed to the concept, most people assume they are left brainers. Why is that? Because most people have a deep reservoir of self-confidence. They assume they are always right. And that anyone who disagrees with them has to be wrong.

"I'm right and you're wrong" is an almost universal attitude of a human brain, and a healthy attitude at that. But how does a person develop such strong beliefs? People assume it must be the result of logical, analytical thinking.

That's not necessarily true. You can be a self-confident right brainer, too. Intuitive thinkers can be just as sure of themselves as logical thinkers. Maybe even more so since they don't need facts to support their conclusions.

Even though your brain is unbalanced, you still use both sides to think while favoring one side or the other, much like a person uses both hands to do manual work while favoring either the left or the right hand.

A person whose brain is too much out of balance, however, is likely to suffer from one of the brain disorders such as autism (on the left) or dyslexia (on the right).

In young children whose brains are still developing, some neuroscientists believe it's possible to permanently correct these disorders by a hemispheric approach, that is, by stimulating one side of the brain more than the other. Brain Balance Centers is a pioneer in this approach.

Managers vs. entrepreneurs.

The left-brain/right-brain concept also helps to explain the difference between entrepreneurs and managers.

Entrepreneurs are invariably right brainers. They are usually "visionaries" who focus on the "big picture," oftentimes suffering in the short term. (A good example of intuitive, holistic thinking.)

History suggests that entrepreneurs may not make good long-term managers. Perhaps it takes a right brainer to get a company off the ground and a left brainer to manage that same company when it does get off the ground.

"Without entrepreneurs," writes Stefan Stern in the *Finan-*

cial Times, "there would be no businesses. But if we always put entrepreneurs in charge, there wouldn't be so many businesses left either."

Battles in the boardroom.

In our years of consulting work, we have participated in many of these battles, and we have the scars to prove it.

There seems to be a common theme to these lost battles. Management argues for ideas and concepts that are just plain "common sense," a reflection of their left-brain thinking.

We argue for ideas and concepts that might not be logical, but intuitively we believe are ideas that will work, a reflection of our right-brain thinking.

Who decides? The deck is stacked. Every marketing decision has to be approved by management.

In this book, we explore twenty-five different areas in which there are a difference of opinion between management thinking and marketing thinking—between left brainers and right brainers.

Not all management people are left brainers, of course, nor are all marketing people right brainers.

One CEO who is obviously a right brainer is Steve Jobs, the business world's greatest presenter. Mr. Jobs disdains market research and is highly visual, two traits of a right brainer.

Diversity in the boardroom.

Many boardroom battles take place between two groups who have the same objectives but think differently. As long as both sides understand each other, this diversity can be a good thing.

We recently completed a consulting session for a client in India. The product went on to become a big success. And the client hired us for a second project.

Later, the chief executive told us he thought our idea was "foolish," yet he used it because he had confidence in us.

That's typical of what needs to happen. If you are a left-brain logical person, you are unlikely to be enthusiastic about marketing concepts developed by right-brain people. They just won't make sense.

It's our hope that management people will take the time to better understand the principles of marketing, especially the difference between common sense and marketing sense.

It's also our hope that marketing people will take the time to better understand why management often rejects their proposals and especially the need to reframe those proposals in logical, verbal, analytical terms.

These are the primary objectives of this book.

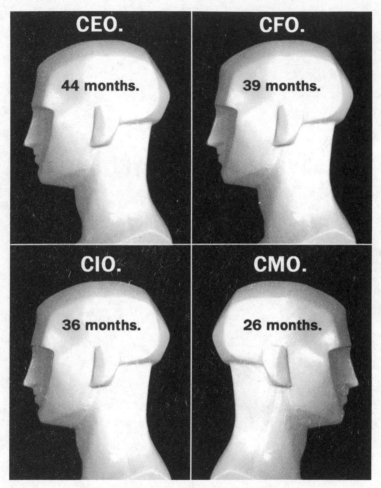

According to a recent Spencer Stuart survey,
a company's chief marketing officer has
the shortest tenure of any top executive.
"This job is radioactive," reported *BusinessWeek*.

Introduction: The Velvet Curtain

From General Electric in New York to the Walt Disney Company in Los Angeles, a velvet curtain has descended across the country separating marketing people from management people.

It's a conundrum. "Marketing is too important," said David Packard, cofounder of Hewlett-Packard, "to be left to the marketing people."

On the other hand, marketing is too complicated to be left to management people who have little experience in marketing and who don't understand its principles.

The gulf between the two.

It's getting wider. It's seriously undermining the cohesiveness that a good team, in business or in sports, needs to be successful.

That ancient motto "All for one and one for all" is seldom heard in the corridors of corporate America today.

In many companies, left-brain management and right-brain

marketing are at war. It's not good for the companies; it's not good for the careers of management or marketing people; it's not good for consumers; and it's not good for the economy.

Deloitte recently conducted 217 in-depth interviews of executives in five European countries. "The majority of CEOs believed their organization understood the role of marketing," reported the accounting firm, "a view that was categorically refuted by the rest of the senior executives and marketing community we surveyed."

Fortune magazine also dramatized the gulf. To celebrate its seventy-fifth anniversary, the publication selected "75 books that teach you everything you really need to know about business."

Apparently, marketing isn't one of those things you really need to know about business because no marketing book made the list.

Take Jack Welch, former CEO of General Electric and *Fortune*'s "Manager of the Century." In his two best-selling books, *Straight from the Gut* and *Winning*, what does the Manager of the Century have to say about marketing?

Almost nothing.

He does, however, have kind words to say about the human resources manager. "The head of HR should be the second most important person in the organization."

(A busy person indeed, replacing all those CMOs who last only twenty-six months on the job.)

Jack Welch did a great job at General Electric. One reason, of course, was that he didn't have to worry much about marketing because GE already had an extremely powerful brand.

Put Mr. Welch in charge of Chrysler and the results would have been much different.

Our sympathies vs. our finances.

As marketing people, our sympathies are with our fellow marketing executives. But our finances are dependent on the chief executive officers of the companies that hire us to help them with their marketing strategies.

As marketing consultants, we have had the pleasure (and pain) of working with hundreds of companies in dozens of different industries. Invariably, it's the CEO who hires us. Invariably, it's the CEO who outlines the problems facing the company. Invariably, it's the CEO who decides whether or not to follow our recommendations.

Where are the company's marketing people in the strategy sessions we conduct? They're generally sitting on one side of the table. On the other side are the company's management people. In between the two sides is the velvet curtain.

This book is our attempt to lift that velvet curtain. To bridge the gap between the two sides. To help explain marketing to management. And management to marketing.

Educating a chief executive.

As marketing consultants, you might think we spend most of our time advising clients on the strategies and tactics to use in their marketing programs. But we don't. We spend most of our time educating management on the principles of marketing.

Most CEOs are exceedingly bright. A dim bulb seldom lights up the corner office. When a CEO understands what marketing can (and cannot) do, the CEO can usually figure out what to do.

Unfortunately, those exceedingly bright CEOs also have an exceedingly warped sense of what marketing is all about.

Unwarping those minds is difficult because almost everything logical, left-brain management people know about marketing is wrong.

Marketing is not common sense, nor is it easy to learn. If it were, there would be no reason to hire a CMO in the first place. Just let the company's commonsense management run the marketing side of the business too.

Company after company gets into trouble because they hire hard-charging CEOs with great knowledge and common sense, but little or no understanding of marketing.

Take Chrysler, for example. In 2006, Chrysler sales fell 7 percent and the company lost $1.5 billion. That's one reason why in 2007 Daimler virtually gave away the company to Cerberus Capital Management.

What did Cerberus do next? They hired Robert Nardelli, the former chief executive of Home Depot, to drive Chrysler out of the ditch.

And what is Mr. Nardelli's expertise? According to newspaper reports, he's a "cost-cutting, manufacturing" expert.

"They got it," Nardelli said of Chrysler management, which plans to cut thirteen thousand jobs. "If we can do it faster, if we can do it more efficiently, that's what we want to do."

Faster? More efficiently? Is that what Chrysler's problem is? Any marketing person knows what Chrysler's problem is. It's not a manufacturing problem, and it's not a pricing problem.

Name one reason to buy a Chrysler. We can't; can you?

Chrysler has a marketing problem.

Making cheaper Chryslers faster is not going to do it. Chrysler products, on a comparative basis, are already less expensive than Toyotas, Hondas, or Nissans.

Chief executives have a hard time recognizing marketing problems. You don't get to be CEO until you first fall in love with your company and then express your everlasting loyalty to your company's brands.

Even an outsider has to first genuflect in the direction of the company's brands.

As Nardelli said when he joined Chrysler, "This is more than financial. This is about trying to bring Chrysler, this unbelievably iconic brand, to its proper place."

You can't solve a problem until you first recognize the problem. What marketing person would ever refer to Chrysler as an "unbelievably iconic brand"?

Mercedes-Benz, maybe. But Chrysler?

From a marketing point of view, most Chrysler brands are a mess. What's a Chrysler? Is it an inexpensive PT Cruiser or an expensive Chrysler 300?

What's a Dodge? Is it a cheap car? Or an expensive truck? Or vice versa?

Yet it's common sense for companies to think they need a full range of products to market under each of their brand names.

When Chrysler bought American Motors years ago, that company also was a mess. The only American Motors brand with a strong perception was Jeep. (And even then, American Motors thought its Jeep dealers also needed to sell passenger cars under the Eagle brand.)

After the acquisition, the only American Motors brand that Chrysler kept was Jeep. The rest were parked in history's garage.

Two different "takes" to every deal.

There's a management take and a marketing take.

When Daimler-Benz bought Chrysler in 1998 for $36 billion, it was, according to the *International Herald Tribune*, ". . . a landmark deal initially hailed as a blueprint for the future of the global auto industry."

What does that sound like to you? To us, it sounds like a typical left-brain management take.

The right-brain marketing take is just the opposite: a German-American car company selling cheap, expensive vehicles?

Intuitively, that doesn't make marketing sense.

It didn't make financial sense, either. After selling Chrysler to Cerberus Capital Management in a complex deal, the $36 billion that Daimler paid for its acquisition, according to our calculations, was worth just $1.6 billion. (Daimler recently wrote down the value of its Chrysler stake to zero.)

Why was the Chrysler acquisition such a disaster for Daimler? It was a management decision made without an understanding of the marketing consequences.

Management people (and their merger-and-acquisition allies) like to put two companies together that *complement* each other. That way, the combination has a larger potential market to shoot for.

True enough, but as marketing people would point out, that kind of merger can destroy brands. DaimlerChrysler was a car company lacking authenticity and a sense of purpose. How could DaimlerChrysler build its brands on such a weak foundation?

(It's like combining Coca-Cola with Eastman Kodak to produce a conglomerate called Coca-Kodak.)

Low prices vs. high prices.

Logical left-brain management wants to build sales. So management's emphasis is on cost cutting and manufacturing expertise.

Intuitive right-brain marketing wants to build brands. Often the best way to build a brand is to make your product more expensive than the competition. That way, you create the perception that your brand must be "better."

(Examples: Starbucks, Red Bull, Absolut, Grey Goose, Rolex, Lexus, Mercedes-Benz, Bose, Dyson, Evian, Grey Poupon, Godiva, and dozens of other brands.)

A higher price is not necessarily a negative. One definition of a brand is a product or service that consumers will pay more for than an equivalent commodity.

If consumers won't pay more for your brand than they would for a commodity, then you really don't have a brand. All you have is a commodity with a name on it.

The early history of Federal Express illustrates the difference between the management approach and the marketing approach—in other words, the difference between competing on "pricing" and competing on "branding."

Early on, Federal Express tried to compete with air-cargo-leader Emery Air Freight by undercutting it on price. Each of Federal Express's three services (overnight, two-day, and three-day) was priced lower than the comparable Emery service.

It didn't work. In the first three years, Federal Express lost $29 million.

Then entrepreneur Fred Smith switched to a branding approach. He narrowed the focus to overnight delivery and increased his advertising budget fivefold, using the slogan "When it absolutely, positively has to be there overnight."

The turnaround was astonishing. Federal Express went on to dominate the overnight-delivery business and became a much larger company than Emery.

The irony is that Federal Express never did give up its two-day and three-day services. These alternatives can still be found on the company's airbills.

Yet from a perception point of view, FedEx is still the "overnight" delivery service.

Expansion vs. contraction.

Management and marketing are poles apart when it comes to evaluating a company's strategy.

Left-brain management's first thought is usually to expand the business. At Home Depot, one of Nardelli's first moves was to expand its building-supply business by acquiring some twenty-five wholesale suppliers. (Home Depot eventually sold that business.)

Right-brain marketing's first thought is usually to narrow the focus. You can't build a brand if you don't stand for something in the consumer's mind. Often the best way to stand for something is to isolate a single service you can dominate or an attribute you can own.

Where would FedEx be today if the company had hired a "cost-cutting, manufacturing expert" as its chief executive officer?

Probably in the same situation as Chrysler.

Let's lift the velvet curtain. Let's get management to understand marketing and marketing to understand management.

In a survey of twelve hundred consumers,
Crystal Pepsi was voted the
"best new grocery product of the year."
Twelve months later, the product was gone.

CHAPTER 1

Management deals in reality. Marketing deals in perception.

The first responsibility of a leader," said Max DePree, former CEO of Herman Miller, "is to define reality."

Management deals in facts and figures, a left-brain analytical approach to a problem. "Getting to the bottom of the situation" is the goal. In short, management deals in reality.

Marketing deals almost exclusively in perception. What matters to marketing people are not the "facts" of a situation, but what's in the minds of consumers that may or may not correspond with reality.

Since perceptions are difficult to measure, marketing people often use right-brain intuitive, holistic thinking.

Management people, of course, are aware of the importance of perception. The problem is they believe perception is a mirror. It's just a reflection of reality. Change the reality and you change the perception.

Marketing people disagree. Changing reality is easy. But changing perception is among the most difficult jobs in the universe.

"This is our surest move ever."

That's what one chief executive said before the launch of a new product that could make or break his company.

That chief executive was Roberto Goizueta, former CEO of Coca-Cola, who confidently predicted the success of New Coke.

How could it miss? The company conducted almost two hundred thousand consumer taste tests that proved conclusively that New Coke tasted better than the original formula.

New Coke was a new, improved product. And doesn't the better product win in the marketplace?

The universal answer to this question in the boardrooms of corporate America is "Yes, of course, the better product wins. That's why we spend millions of dollars benchmarking our competitors. We won't launch a new product until we can develop a definitive competitive advantage."

That's reality at work in left-brain management circles. That's also why the vast majority of new supermarket and drugstore products fail in America today.

"The best idea I've ever had . . . "

That's what David Novak, now CEO of Yum! Brands, said about Crystal Pepsi. And, he quickly added, it was "the worst executed."

"Crystal Pepsi was an idea that was well ahead of its time," said Mr. Novak. "It was a brilliant idea."

Nor did he let Crystal Pepsi's failure undermine his confidence in his ability to predict the future. "We could have been clearer in the positioning to have it taste a little more like Pepsi, like people suggested, and it would have been a home run."

Crystal Pepsi hit the supermarkets in 1992, a year when the "clear craze" was sweeping the country.

Also introduced that year was Miller Clear. At the launch of the product, one of the brand managers said, "If you close your eyes, you would think you were drinking regular beer."

An editor attending the press function replied, "Tastes like regular beer *only* if I close my eyes?"

Clear beer, clear cola, clear toothpaste, clear mouthwash, clear dishwashing detergent, clear window cleaner, clear deodorant, clear antiperspirant, clear cosmetics, clear gasoline, and dozens of other clear products were launched into the market.

None of these clear products made much of an impact.

Actually, Miller Clear only tasted like regular beer if you *did* close your eyes. When you drank Miller Clear with your eyes wide open, it tasted like watery beer. Perception always trumps reality.

What keeps bad ideas alive at the management level is the disconnect between strategy and execution. The CEO who dreams up the bad idea can always blame the execution.

"The best idea I've ever had and the worst executed." Many management people, many politicians, and many motion-picture producers can say exactly the same thing. And do.

The irony is that the "red color" in a cola drink is just a dye added to the mixture before it's bottled. No matter.

The perception in the consumer's mind is that a cola product has to be reddish-brown. You putter with this perception at your own peril.

Crystal Pepsi a home run? It could taste exactly like regular Pepsi and still strike out. That's marketing's point of view.

AL & LAURA RIES

"The most compelling luxury vehicle currently sold."

A pet project of Volkswagen supervisory board chairman Ferdinand Piech, the luxury Phaeton model was introduced in 2003 and received exceptionally good reviews.

"It might be the most-compelling luxury vehicle currently sold," reported *Business 2.0* magazine, "It is overwhelmingly the best value among high-end luxury cars. Without question it is a magnificent vehicle."

Volkswagen recently announced it was withdrawing its Phaeton model from the U.S. market. No surprise there. Since its introduction in November 2003, VW has sold just 3,354 Phaetons in the United States.

Why would Volkswagen, a company known for small, relatively inexpensive cars, introduce the Phaeton, a sedan that started at $68,655 for the V-8 model and went up to $100,255 for the twelve-cylinder version?

Reality at work. With the low end of the market being taken over by brands from Japan and Korea (Toyota, Honda, Nissan, Mazda, Hyundai, Kia, and others), the folks at Volkswagen figured they would have to move upmarket.

Furthermore, low-cost Chinese brands are poised to enter the American market. With all this competition at the low end, it makes sense for Volkswagen to get into bigger, more-expensive, and presumably more-profitable cars. That's left-brain logic at work.

Hence the Phaeton, a model that would not only stake out a claim at the high end, but whose success would also add luster to the rest of the Volkswagen product line.

We can visualize what happened in the boardroom. Grown men, with decades of experience in the automobile field, sat around a conference table and decided to launch a Volkswagen vehicle with a price tag reaching six digits.

(We don't know any right-brain marketer who would have thought that was a good idea.)

Forbes called the Phaeton "a great car." *USA Today* gave it a glowing review: "Styling is nice. The interior decor sets a standard for class and taste. Comfort is exceptional. Driving personality is ever-so-lovely. Power's right."

"And yet the company can't give them away," concluded *Business 2.0.* "Blame two minor faults: a VW badge on the front grille, and another on the trunk."

That's perception at work.

Wal-Mart moves up the fashion ladder.

What happened at Volkswagen also happened at Wal-Mart. Management thinks, "We're getting a reputation for selling nothing but cheap merchandise."

So what did Wal-Mart do? "We can move upscale," thinks left-brain management. So the company hired a top executive from Target, opened an office in Manhattan's Fashion District, presented a fashion show in New York City, ran an eight-page advertisement in *Vogue,* and started selling diamond rings, some costing as much as $9,988. (Phaeton owners now had a reason to shop at Wal-Mart.)

Nothing worked. "Wal-Mart's fashion faux pas," reported the *Wall Street Journal.* "Discounter's effort to upgrade style falls flat. . . . Stacks of unsold clothing are clogging store aisles and pressuring profits."

The top merchant who oversaw the discount chain's ill-fated foray into fashionable clothing and home decor resigned.

Recently, Wal-Mart announced it was changing its logotype. "WAL-MART" is now "Walmart" with a yellow starburst. If new stylish clothing can't change the perception of the brand, maybe a new stylish logotype might accomplish the same thing.

This is wishful thinking on management's part. When a brand has been around as long as Wal-Mart has and when a brand has achieved as much awareness as Wal-Mart has, nothing is going to change the perception of the brand. Consumers are just going to associate the new logo with their old perceptions.

Management people approach every situation in a sane, sensible way. Their emphasis is always on the product. "If we can produce a better product at a better price, we can win the marketing battle."

Marketing people approach every situation from the prospect's point of view. Their emphasis is on perception. "How do we improve sales by taking advantage of the perception of the brand?"

The "everybody knows" problem.

This is what makes marketing doubly difficult. For example, when you ask an automobile buyer about the difference between Japanese and American cars, he or she is likely to say, "*Everybody knows* that Japanese vehicles are superior to American vehicles."

Those buyers may not have any experience with American cars at all, but they will still believe that Japanese vehicles are superior. Even if the buyers have had some experience with both American and Japanese vehicles, they still might cling to their original perceptions.

If a Japanese vehicle has problems, the owner might think, "Well, it's just one of those things that seldom happen." If an American vehicle has problems, the owner might think, "Well, they just don't build them the way they do in Japan."

Perception wins again. But that's not left-brain management's point of view.

Predicted reliability of automotive brands.

1. Toyota	19. BMW
2. Honda	20. Pontiac
3. Scion	21. Chevrolet
4. Acura	22. Dodge
5. Lexus	23. Chrysler
6. Subaru	24. Nissan
7. Hyundai	25. Saab
8. Infiniti	26. Suzuki
9. Mitsubishi	27. Volkswagen
10. Mercury	28. Mini
11. Mazda	29. Porsche
12. Audi	30. Saturn
13. Lincoln	31. Cadillac
14. GMC	32. Jeep
15. Volvo	33. Jaguar
16. Ford	34. Hummer
17. Kia	35. Land Rover
18. Buick	36. Mercedes-Benz

In a 2007 survey of "predicted reliability,"
Consumer Reports ranked Mercedes-Benz
dead last among 36 major automobile brands.
It didn't matter; Mercedes sales went up.

CHAPTER 2

Management concentrates on the product. Marketing concentrates on the brand.

In 1989, General Motors was the largest company in the world with sales of $127 billion. It made more money ($4.2 billion) and had more assets ($173 billion) than any other company.

Then things started to go downhill. In 1992, just three years later, General Motors managed to lose $23.5 billion.

Today, on the stock market, General Motors is worth just $1.8 billion. Toyota is worth more than sixty-one times as much ($110.7 billion.)

What happened to General Motors? According to management experts, according to automotive analysts, according to the trade press, the problem was obvious. The corporation didn't build cars that people wanted to buy.

"It's still product, product, product."

That was the headline of a recent column written by the publisher of *Automotive News*, the industry's bible.

In his column, he wrote: "There are examples of great products that changed the future for a car company. There also are examples of product that contributed to a slow, quiet death for a company. The continual erosion of market share is a function of product.

"It proves again that in the automobile business, nothing matters except the product," concluded the publisher.

Nothing matters except the product? That's typical left-brain management thinking.

It sounds so logical, how could anyone disagree?

But when you look at the situation from a car buyer's point of view, the "better-product" logic falls apart.

One could trudge through the showrooms of Ford, Chevrolet, Dodge, Toyota, Honda, and Nissan dealerships and compare the vehicles. But for what purpose?

Even an automotive expert would be hard pressed to find any significant quality differences.

There are significant differences, of course, but they don't exist in the product. They exist in the mind of the buyer.

- If the prospect wants a cheap car, he or she heads to a Hyundai or Kia dealership.
- A well-built car? Toyota.
- A sport-utility vehicle? Jeep.
- A car that's fun to drive? BMW.
- A car that's safe to drive? Volvo.
- A luxurious Japanese car? Lexus.
- A prestigious car? Mercedes-Benz.
- A sports car? Porsche.

Are there quality differences between successful vehicles and unsuccessful ones? Maybe, but who's to judge? The car buyer can't. And the car buyer often doesn't pay attention to rating services like *Consumer Reports*.

Take Mercedes-Benz, for example.

In the U.S. market, Mercedes has increased its sales every year for the last fourteen years in a row—from 61,899 vehicles in 1993 to 253,277 vehicles in 2007, an increase of 309 percent.

These increases were in spite of some pretty negative stories in the media about the reliability of the brand.

AN ENGINEERING ICON SLIPS
Quality ratings for Mercedes drop in several surveys.
—*Wall Street Journal*, FEBRUARY 4, 2002

MERCEDES' HEAD-ON COLLISION WITH A QUALITY SURVEY
—*BusinessWeek*, JULY 21, 2003

MERCEDES HITS A POTHOLE
Owner complaints are up. Resale values are down.
—*Fortune*, OCTOBER 27, 2003

So what? Mercedes-Benz is a better automobile *brand*, if not a better automobile *product*.

How times have changed.

In 1989, when General Motors was king of automotive hill, Cadillac outsold Mercedes 3.5 to 1 (266,899 units versus 76,152).

In 2007, Mercedes outsold Cadillac 253,277 to 214,726, a feat all the more remarkable considering that Mercedes vehicles generally sell for more money than Cadillacs.

Remember when Cadillac meant something? Remember when the "Cadillac of the category" was a compliment applied to many different brands in many different categories?

No longer. Cadillac is just another automobile brand overtaken by a competitor with a superior strategy.

No wonder General Motors is in trouble. In 2005, General Motors lost $10.6 billion. In 2006, GM lost $2.0 billion. In 2007, GM lost $38.7 billion.

Ford is also in trouble. In the last three years, the company lost $13.9 billion.

Management often blames the high cost of health care and retirement benefits for the problems of the U.S. automotive industry. But consider Daimler AG.

One of the most expensive countries in the world to manufacture anything is Germany. According to a recent survey by accounting firm KPMG, it costs 17 percent more to manufacture something in Germany than it does in the United States. Furthermore, Daimler has to pay for shipping some of those Mercedes-Benz cars and parts across the North Atlantic.

In spite of its high costs, in spite of the burden of carrying its money-losing Chrysler division, Daimler managed to make $13.5 billion in net profits the last three years.

Mercedes is just a better *brand* than Cadillac.

Better product vs. better brand.

Almost by definition, a better product is essentially similar to competition except that it's "better" in some measurable way. Coca-Cola and Pepsi-Cola are essentially similar except that taste tests prove that Pepsi tastes better than Coke.

It doesn't matter. Coca-Cola outsells Pepsi in the U.S. market by more than 50 percent. (And its lead overseas is even greater.)

Coca-Cola is just a better *brand* than Pepsi-Cola.

Why? Coca-Cola was the first cola in the minds of consumers. As a result, it's perceived as "the real thing." The original, authentic cola.

You don't build a better brand by being *better* than the competition. You build a better brand by being *different* than the competition.

When Mercedes-Benz arrived in the American market, its cars were considerably more expensive than Cadillacs. The high prices created the perception that the Mercedes brand was somehow superior to the Cadillac brand.

In other words, in a class by itself.

(Nicely reinforced by Mercedes's longtime advertising theme: "Engineered like no other car in the world.")

As a result of its high prices, Mercedes sales took off slowly. Here are annual sales of Mercedes cars, a decade apart.

1954: 1,000 (the number imported, not all of which were
    sold that year)
1964: 11,234
1974: 38,826
1984: 79,222
1994: 73,002

After forty years in the American market, Mercedes was still selling fewer vehicles in a year than Chevrolet was selling in a month. No wonder General Motors wasn't particularly concerned.

But Mercedes was building a brand that was going to pay enormous dividends down the road.

What Mercedes did in automobiles, Absolut did in vodka. By pricing the brand 50 percent higher than the best-selling Smirnoff vodka, Absolut created a new category that ultimately became known as "premium" vodka.

What Absolut did to Smirnoff, Grey Goose did to Absolut. By pricing the brand 60 percent higher than Absolut, Grey Goose became known as the "ultra-premium" vodka.

Seven years after its introduction, entrepreneur Sidney Frank sold Grey Goose to Bacardi Ltd. for $2 billion.

And Vin & Sprit, a Swedish company whose major brand is Absolut vodka, was recently sold to Pernod Ricard of France for $8.9 billion. Not bad for a liquor that by law must be "colorless, odorless and tasteless."

Moving marketing thinking up the organization.

The velvet curtain that divides management from marketing keeps this from happening.

With the enormous worldwide success of its Mercedes brand, you might think that German management would get the message that the brand is more important than the product. And one of the most important ways to send a branding message is to make sure the product is priced right.

No so. According to *Automotive News,* the Daimler board member in charge of the Mercedes group said, "The price tag is not the defining characteristic of the Mercedes brand. It's quality and technology."

Quality and technology?

That's the apparent justification for the launch in Europe of the relatively cheap A-class Mercedes. In the United States, Mercedes-Benz has been promoting its low-end C-class models with advertising messages such as "Built like a Mercedes. Performs like a Mercedes. Priced like a regular car."

Regular cars are priced like regular cars. Luxury cars are priced like luxury cars. That's a marketing principle Mercedes management seems to have missed.

When you have a strong brand like Mercedes, you can make many mistakes and still come out ahead. Compare General Motors and Ford with Daimler AG.

In a recent year, General Motors and Ford sold 14.7 million vehicles worldwide, more than three times the volume of Daimler AG (4.7 million). Yet on the stock market, Daimler is worth $27.5 billion, more than four times the value of General Motors ($1.8 billion) and Ford ($4.4 billion) combined.

What should Cadillac have done? It should have moved upscale to block the Mercedes brand. Instead, it moved downscale with models like the Cimarron and the Catera.

You don't make money building better products; you make money building better brands.

Howdy, Audi.

No automotive brand has introduced as many advanced technological features as Audi, a division of Volkswagen. Some Audi innovations include all-wheel drive, direct fuel injection, the advanced design of the TT coupe and roadster, and the twelve-cylinder, aluminum-bodied A8.

The goal, according to chairman Martin Winterkorn: "Audi AG wants to be the leading premium brand worldwide by 2010."

And in 2007, Johan de Nysschen, executive vice president of Audi of America, said he wants to turn Audi into a sophisticated, edgy, luxury brand for the U.S. market as it shoots for a long-term sales goal of two hundred thousand vehicles a year by 2015.

Toward that goal, Audi just introduced the $110,000, 420-horsepower, space-frame R8 sports car, the $82,675, 420-horsepower RS cabriolet, and the $51,275, 354-horsepower S5 sports coupe. The sports cars, according to Marc Trahan, Audi's number two U.S. executive, "help to further strengthen and clarify what Audi is all about."

Audi, in our opinion, is not going to be the leading premium brand worldwide by 2010. Nor is Audi going to sell two hundred thousand vehicles in the United States by 2015.

In the thirty-four years that Audi has been selling cars in America, it has never sold more than 100,000 units a year. In 2007, sales were just 93,506 units, fewer than Suzuki, which sold 101,884 vehicles.

In the automobile field, what matters is the brand, not the product. And Audi is a weak brand for two reasons: (1) Unlike Mercedes-Benz, Audi was not the first "expensive" automobile brand in the American market, and (2) Audi, at least in America, is almost as bad a name as Suzuki.

When it comes to names, left-brain management people seem to have a tin ear. Audi? Suzuki? These names just don't have the poetry of "Mercedes-Benz."

Sayonara Isuzu.

"Lying Joe" Isuzu once was as famous as Britney, Lindsay, or Paris. *Advertising Age* selected the Joe Isuzu program as the eighty-third best advertising campaign of the twentieth century, one notch ahead of "The ultimate driving machine."

In spite of Lying Joe's celebrity status, Isuzu has dropped out of the U.S. market. Sales were dismal. In 2007, only 7,098 Isuzus were sold in America.

What went wrong at Isuzu? According to one report, "The cause of its death: failure to innovate, misjudgment of the market and woeful underspending on marketing." (A typical logical explanation of the problem.)

But what about the Isuzu name? Every time a brand with a bad name bites the dust, left-brain management types never blame the name. They always blame the product.

Right-brain marketing types consider an automobile to be like a bottle of beer. It's a badge you wear that tells people who you are and what you stand for.

"I drive a BMW" makes a statement to your friends and neighbors. "I drive an Isuzu." What does that say about your status in life?

You can't make a statement with a name like "Isuzu." Consumers can't spell it; consumers can't pronounce it. (The name is pronounced "e-suzu," not "i-suzu.")

Isuzu isn't the first imported car with a bad name to drop out of the American market. Peugeot dropped out in 1991, Yugo in 1992, Daihatsu in 1993, Daewoo in 2002.

Isuzu, Daewoo, Daihatsu, Yugo, and Peugeot. What do these names have in common? To an English-speaking person, these names are not euphonious. They sound bad.

(There are still a number of brands with dubious names struggling to make a mark in the American automobile market. To name four: Suzuki, Subaru, Saab, and Mitsubishi.)

Would it surprise you to learn that Isuzu sold 650,734

vehicles in 2007? (Isuzu Motors Ltd. is the eighteenth-largest automobile manufacturer in the world.)

The company just didn't happen to sell many of those vehicles in the United States, the largest automobile market in the world. It did happen to sell a lot of those vehicles in countries where English is not the spoken language.

The name is the foundation of a marketing program. You can't build a brand with a weak name. It's like building a house on sand.

Current sales vs. current perceptions.

Just because a company sells millions of dollars worth of products a year doesn't make the company (or its brands) strong. In the long run, what counts are current perceptions, not current sales.

There are many companies with substantial current sales but weak current perceptions. Eventually, these weak perceptions will undermine both the companies' sales and the companies' financial strengths.

Take Chevrolet and Ford, the two leading U.S. automobile brands. Both brands continue to sell millions of cars and trucks a year. But these are weak brands propped up by three factors.

1. There are far more Chevrolet and Ford cars on the highways than any other brand. When an owner of one of these cars decides to trade it in, his or her first thought is to buy another of the same make.

Why? Maybe the hope of a better trade-in allowance. Or a good relationship with a salesperson. Or the dealership happens to be close by.

2. There are far more Chevrolet and Ford dealerships than any other brand.

Chevrolet has 3,976 franchises. Ford has 3,602 franchises.

Toyota has only 1,228. Not surprisingly, the average Toyota dealer sells more than twice as many cars and trucks as the average Chevrolet dealer.

3. There are far-higher incentives available at Chevrolet and Ford dealerships. In a recent month, the average General Motors dealer was offering an incentive of $3,858 per vehicle. Ford, $3,410 per vehicle. And all the Japanese car makers combined, $929 per vehicle on average.

A number of years ago, General Motors hired Robert Lutz (a former Chrysler and Ford executive) to put pizzazz into the design and function of GM products. And he has. Automotive gurus have lauded the Aura, Malibu, Solstice, Sky, CTS, and other GM vehicles.

There's nothing wrong with the cars. It's the branding that's wrong.

When General Motors had half of the U.S. automobile market, it also had a finely tuned marketing strategy. Chevrolet was its entry-level car. And then you moved up the ladder to Pontiac, Oldsmobile, Buick and Cadillac.

Except for Cadillac, today's GM branding ladder goes nowhere. Moving from Chevrolet to Pontiac to Buick is essentially a sideways move. The three brands are all competing with the same portfolio of vehicles.

(Years ago, Pontiac was the Pepsi-Cola of cars, a brand focused on the younger generation. You would have thought, would you not, that GM would have given its youth-oriented car, the Corvette, to Pontiac instead of Chevrolet?)

What is GM's entry-level car? Saturn or Chevrolet? The answer is both, which is not good right-brain marketing thinking.

Years ago, Al was invited to visit Buick, where he was taken through the design studio. "What are they doing over there?" he asked.

"They're designing our entry-level Buick," someone said.

"Your entry-level Buick," Al replied, "is Chevrolet."

The futility of a better-product strategy.

Consider Microsoft Windows, with a worldwide share of the personal-computer operating-system market of more than 90 percent. How is the number two brand, Apple's Macintosh, going to compete with Windows?

By building a better operating system? Macintosh already has the better operating system. Here's what the country's foremost technology expert (Walter Mossberg of the *Wall Street Journal*) has to say: "Macs have better hardware, a better operating system and better bundled software than Windows PCs."

Even with better hardware, a better operating system, and better-bundled software, Apple has only about 5 percent of the worldwide market.

How would you compete with Heinz ketchup? By making a better-tasting ketchup?

How would you compete with Tabasco pepper sauce? By making a better-tasting pepper sauce?

It's not a better product or service that makes a strong brand. It's the brand's market share. Brands like McDonald's, Starbucks, Rolex, and many other brands are powerful because they dominate their market segments.

Does McDonald's make a better hamburger than Burger King? (When we worked for Burger King, their research showed otherwise.)

Does Starbucks make better coffee than McDonald's does in its specialty coffee bars? (*Consumer Reports* said no.)

Does Rolex make a better watch than dozens of other luxury-watch makers?

Perhaps. Perhaps not. But a tangible difference in product quality is rarely a factor in the continuing success of a leading brand. Over time, most brands in a category tend to be quite similar. The differences noticed by the consumer are created by the brands themselves.

Perception dictates reality. Starbucks coffee tastes better because the consumer thinks Starbucks coffee tastes better.

The larger the market share, the more dominant the brand, the greater effect the brand has on the consumer's perception of reality.

Consumers consider all candy bars pretty much alike, because no one brand dominates the candy-bar category.

Consumers don't consider all ketchup alike because Heinz dominates the ketchup category. ("Heinz must be better," thinks the consumer. "It's the leading brand.")

Every 1 percent increase in a brand's market share does two things, both favorable: (1) it increases the power of the brand in the mind of the consumer, and (2) it decreases the power of competitive brands.

Left-brain management wants to build a better product. Right-brain marketing wants to build a more dominant brand.

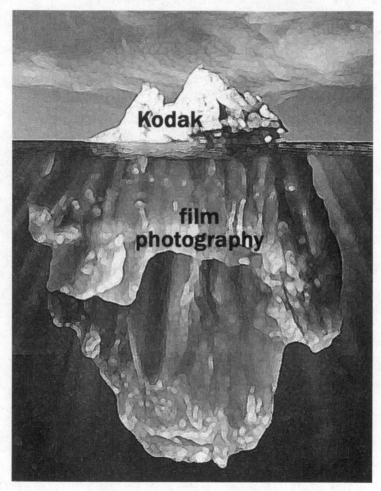

When film photography was dominant,
Kodak was an exceptionally strong brand.
As the category melts, so does the brand.
Today, Kodak is a weak brand.

CHAPTER 3

Management wants to own the brand. Marketing wants to own the category.

While management is focused on building better products, they don't ignore brands. Quite the contrary.

Management has jumped on the branding bandwagon and started to claim the concept as its own.

One of the most widely read issues of *BusinessWeek* is its annual report on the top one hundred global brands and their estimated values.

The perennial leader is Coca-Cola, worth $66.7 billion in 2008. In second place was IBM, worth $59.0 billion. In third place was Microsoft, also worth $59.0 billion.

Numbers like these grab management's attention. No wonder many chief executives equate a company's potential with the value of its brand.

A brand is the tip of an iceberg.

The iceberg is the category. How big and how deep the iceberg is will determine how valuable the brand is.

It's easy to confuse the category with the brand. "What would you like to drink?" a waiter might ask. The consumer thinks, "Do I want a beer, a cocktail, a glass of wine, a soft drink?"

After a moment's thought, the consumer might say, "I'd like a Coke."

The brand is the visible face of the category. But the consumer's first decision is the selection of the category. The brand always follows that choice.

Consumers think categories, but they frequently express their category choices in terms of brands. It might seem like the brand is the dominant decision when it's not.

Categories and brands are locked together. If the iceberg melts, the brand will melt, too. That's why most right-brain marketing people are concerned with the category first and the brand second.

Take Kodak, for example. In 1999, Interbrand ranked Kodak as the sixteenth most valuable brand in the world, worth $14.8 billion.

Every year since, the Kodak brand has fallen in both rank and value. In 2007, Interbrand ranked Kodak number eighty-two, worth just $3.9 billion. (In 2008, Kodak didn't make the list.)

In eight years, 74 percent of the Kodak iceberg melted away.

What's a Kodak?

It's the world's best film-photography brand. Unfortunately for Kodak, the world is turning to digital photography.

Years ago, we were discussing the situation with a Kodak executive. It was no secret then that digital photography was starting to replace film. You're going to have to launch a second brand, we said.

Not so, the executive replied. The Kodak brand stands for more than just film. It stands for "trust."

Consumers trust Kodak for film photography, so why wouldn't they trust Kodak for digital photography? That makes a lot of sense to a left brainer.

Sense doesn't matter in marketing. The Kodak name was the tip of the film-photography iceberg. And so far no brand, including Kodak, has managed to climb to the top of the digital-photography iceberg.

As a matter of fact, all of the digital camera brands (Sony, Nikon, Olympus, Pentax, Casio, Samsung, Panasonic, etc.) are line extensions from other icebergs.

(There's something wrong when a company called Fujifilm Holdings introduces the Fujifilm digital camera.)

Nobody is thinking category. Everybody is thinking brand. "How do we take advantage of our well-known brand to carve out a piece of this new iceberg?"

The Eastman Kodak Company has been devastated by its brand-oriented approach. In the last seven years of the twentieth century (1994 to 2000), the company had sales of $104.1 billion and net profits after taxes of $7.3 billion, or a 7 percent net profit margin.

In the first seven years of the twenty-first century (2001 to 2007), Eastman Kodak had sales of $90.7 billion and net profits of $380 million, or just 0.4 percent net profit margin.

(The stock market has also lost its trust in the Kodak brand.)

What's puzzling about the Kodak situation is the fact that back in 1976, the company invented the digital camera. If Kodak had given its invention a new brand name, it could have been a big winner.

Dominating a category.

That's the real objective of a marketing program. A brand that doesn't dominate a category is generally a weak brand.

Red Bull dominates the energy-drink category. Starbucks dominates the high-end coffee category. Google dominates the search category. The Body Shop dominates the natural-cosmetics category. Whole Foods dominates the organic-food category. BlackBerry dominates the wireless-e-mail category.

Does it surprise you that all of these relatively recent brand successes were started by entrepreneurs, not by established companies?

It shouldn't. Big companies are busy burnishing their brands, while entrepreneurs are looking for ways to dominate new categories. Big companies think brands. Entrepreneurs think categories.

Brands are important, but they have value only to the extent they stand for categories. The world's most valuable brand, according to Interbrand, is Coca-Cola. But the value of the Coca-Cola brand has been steadily falling. In 1999, it was worth $83.8 billion. In 2008, it was worth only $66.7 billion.

Why is the Coke brand falling in value?

Because the cola iceberg is melting. Since the millennium, per capita consumption of carbonated soft drinks in the United States has fallen 1 or 2 percent each year. This slow decline has been happening in spite of the more than $300 million spent annually on Coca-Cola advertising.

As an iceberg melts, so does its brand.

In 1993, according to Interbrand, Marlboro was the world's most valuable brand, worth $47 billion. In 2008, the brand was worth only $21 billion.

As the smoking iceberg melts, the Marlboro brand is someday going to be essentially worthless.

As the minicomputer disappeared, so did the value of the Digital Equipment brand. As the word processor disappeared, so did the value of the Wang brand. As instant photography disappeared, so did the value of the Polaroid brand.

Many left-brain executives are so brand oriented that their first thought is "How do I save my brand?"

So Digital Equipment launched a line of personal computers with the Digital name. And Wang launched a line of personal computers with the Wang name.

And Polaroid launched a raft of new products, including conventional cameras and film, printers, scanners, medical imaging systems, security systems, videotapes, and so on. All with the Polaroid name, of course.

All for naught. Polaroid went bankrupt in 2001 and, through a series of transactions, wound up in the hands of the Petters Group in 2005.

That year, when the new chairman was asked what Polaroid would be like in the year 2010, he replied, "It's a consumer electronics leader known for really cool products that offer quality and value."

In the consumer ocean, there's no iceberg named "cool products that offer quality and value in consumer electronics." So expect Polaroid's second reincarnation to be no more successful than its first one.

Two types of icebergs.

The first type is narrow and deep. The second type is broad and shallow. While the second type might offer greater sales potential, the first type offers greater profit potential and greater brand stability.

(Just like a boat with a deep keel is more stable than one with a shallow keel.)

Brands that are narrow and deep are almost invulnerable to competitive attacks. Furthermore, they usually are incredibly profitable. Think Rolex in expensive watches, for example.

There are many other brands that also fit this description.

- Hellmann's in mayonnaise
- Tabasco in pepper sauce
- Planters' in peanuts
- WD-40 in "slippery"
- Band-Aid in adhesive bandages
- Q-tips in cotton swabs
- Clorox in bleach
- Ikea in unassembled furniture

When an iceberg melts, left brainers will generally try to save the brand. That's logical, but it's not a good strategy. Better to look around for a new iceberg that is just forming.

Then launch a new brand to dominate that incipient iceberg. That's what a right brainer would do.

Pepsi-Cola wins.

Coca-Cola wins.

In blind taste tests, consumers prefer
Pepsi to Coke. When they can see
what they're drinking, they prefer Coke.
Better products don't necessarily win.

Management demands better products. Marketing demands different products.

Six Sigma and benchmarking are terms you are unlikely to hear in a marketing meeting. But these are very popular terms with left-brain management.

Who could argue with benchmarking your products against the competition? Who could argue with using Six Sigma practices to improve quality by reducing defects to less than 3.4 parts per million?

Management wants to build better products more efficiently and at lower costs. There's nothing wrong with that, but that's not how a company achieves market leadership.

What leaders actually did.

Dell didn't become the leading seller of personal computers by being better than IBM. Dell became the leading seller of personal computers by being different. Dell sold its PCs direct instead of through retail chains.

Amazon didn't become the leading seller of books by being better than Barnes & Noble. Amazon became the leading seller of books by being different. Amazon sold its books on the Internet instead of through retail stores.

Enterprise didn't become the leading car-rental company by being better than Hertz. Enterprise became the leading car-rental company by being different. Enterprise started in the suburbs instead of in airport terminals.

Meanwhile, Avis was busy trying to be better than Hertz. "We try harder" is their approach, but the company never came close to surpassing Hertz.

"We try harder" is the management mantra of many companies in many different countries of the world.

Literally thousands of also-rans are trying to overtake established leaders with a "better-product" or a "better-service" strategy.

"Better" almost never works. Consider these five classic battles.

- Burger King versus McDonald's.
- Energizer versus Duracell.
- Pepsi-Cola versus Coca-Cola.
- *Newsweek* versus *Time*.
- MasterCard versus Visa.

In the history of business, it's extremely rare for a No. 2 company to overtake a market leader by being better. Burger King, Energizer, Pepsi-Cola, Newsweek, MasterCard, and many other companies are doomed to languish in second place unless they change their strategies.

Leaders rarely lose their leadership.

A classic study compared the leading brands in twenty-five different consumer categories in the year 1923 with the leading brands in those same categories today. Just five of the twenty-five brands lost their leadership.

And four of those five didn't lose their leadership to a better product.

- Eveready didn't lose its appliance-battery leadership to a better zinc-carbon battery. Eveready lost its leadership to a different product, the alkaline battery introduced by Duracell.
- Kellogg's didn't lose its cereal leadership to a better corn-flake. Kellogg's lost its cereal leadership to a different product, oat cereal in an unusual shape called Cheerios.
- Ivory didn't lose its facial-soap leadership to a product that was 100 percent pure instead of just 99 and 44/100 percent pure. Ivory lost its facial-soap leadership to Dove, the first soap that was one-quarter "moisturizing lotion."
- Palmolive didn't lose its bath-soap leadership to a better bath soap. Palmolive lost its bath-soap leadership to Dial, the first "deodorant soap."

The fifth loser, Manhattan shirts, is a different story. In fashion categories, the leading brands will all eventually lose their leadership. The essence of fashion is the search for the "new and different," including new and different brands.

The video-game battle.

Three companies are fighting it out: Sony, Microsoft, and Nintendo.

Both Sony's PlayStation 3 and Microsoft's Xbox 360 are the result of a better-product approach. Compared to previous iterations of these video-game consoles, PlayStation 3 and Xbox 360 are faster and more powerful, and contain more features. (Sony's PS3 can even play Blu-ray high-definition movie disks.)

Nintendo did it differently. The Wii is perhaps one-tenth as powerful as its two rivals, yet its motion-sensitive wireless controller allows you to produce action on the screen by tilting and waving your hand. You don't just sit on the couch and move your thumbs.

Wii has been winning the battle in the marketplace. As of April 2008, Nintendo has sold 24.5 million Wii units globally compared with 18 million for Xbox 360 and 10.5 million for PlayStation 3.

Wii has also been winning the battle in the media.

"Nintendo's Wii, radiating fun, is eclipsing Sony."
—*New York Times*

". . . we found the more modest Wii to be the more exciting, fun and satisfying of the two new game machines."—Walter Mossberg, *Wall Street Journal*

"Gamers: Wii has PS3 beat."—*USA Today*

If you want to compete with an established leader, do it differently. In *Sky* magazine, Steven Kent wrote: "Wii compares to 360 and PlayStation 3 in about the same way that a motorcycle compares to an automobile."

A Sony spokesman said essentially the same thing: Wii did not belong in the same category as the more powerful PlayStation 3. (That's good, Sony. Not bad.)

The portable video-game battle.

This would not be the first time Nintendo has won big with a "different" strategy. In 1989, the company introduced Game Boy, the first portable video-game player. Since its introduction, the company has dominated the portable category, selling more than 70 million units.

Several years ago, Sony struck back with the PlayStation Portable, a video-game player with a "better" approach. With the bigger, more powerful PSP, you could also play movies and music in a new propriety format, the Universal Media Disk.

Sony had high hopes for PSP. "The Walkman of the 21st century" is how Sony Computer's CEO described its new machine.

Nintendo did it differently. Instead of introducing a bigger, more powerful Game Boy, Nintendo introduced the DS, a dual-screen portable video-game player. One screen is a regular LCD and the other is a touch-sensitive screen, allowing for a new breed of games.

The Nintendo DS is greatly outselling the PlayStation Portable. In Japan, for example, Nintendo has sold 22.6 million DS machines compared to just 9.3 million for PlayStation Portable.

A marker for the category.

People who want to buy an expensive watch go shopping for a Rolex. People who want to buy a high-capacity MP3 player go shopping for an iPod. People who want to buy an expensive Japanese car go shopping for a Lexus.

In other words, a strong brand owns its category: Silk in soy milk; Netflix in rental DVDs by mail; eBay in Internet auctions; Amazon in Internet books.

Creating a new category and then branding that category in such a way that your brand is perceived as the innovator and category leader (in both senses of the word) is the essence of the right-brain marketing approach.

To create a new category, however, you have to think "different," not "better." Pepsi-Cola tastes better than Coca-Cola, but it's not different and therefore can never become the cola market leader.

Many companies that strive to become market leaders ignore this fundamental principle. This is especially true of smaller companies run by management types with little or no marketing help.

The importance of the name.

Even when a company does think differently, it often misses an opportunity to become the market leader by giving its new brand a line-extension name.

A new category needs a new brand name. But a left brainer at a smaller company thinks, "We can't afford the costs of launching a new brand. So let's use our existing name. Furthermore, we already have some good consumer recognition. With a new brand, we'd have to start all over again. We don't have the resources to launch a new product and a new brand name at the same time, nor is it necessary to launch a new brand."

By circular reasoning, it's easy to prove that "the better product wins."

1. It's an axiom that the better product wins.

2. The leading brand in the category must be the better product.

3. How do we know that? Because the better product always wins.

4. Proving once again that the better product wins in the marketplace. This is left-brain logic at work.

Even the *Automotive News* publisher who stated that "nothing matters except the product" completes the circle by also saying, "Winners and losers are decided in dealership showrooms across the nation when the prospect walks through the door. Nothing else matters."

Translation: How do we know which products are better? *The ones that win in the showrooms.*

Life is not perfect.

In a perfect world, perhaps the better product would always win. But that's not the world we live in.

With thousands of products to choose from in hundreds of different categories, are consumers going to actually buy and compare all the available products in any one category? We think not.

The average supermarket in America has some forty-five thousand individual products for sale. How many of these will the average consumer buy over the course of a year? A hundred? Two hundred? Maybe four hundred at most. (That's still only 1 percent of the items for sale.)

Very, very little comparison shopping actually takes place. Most consumers buy the leading brands. Some buy the cheapest brands. Some buy the brands with unique attributes.

Many private-label products are made by the same companies that make the leading brands. In many cases, the products are the same; the only difference is that the private-label products are cheaper.

Yet most consumers still prefer the leading brands. The power lies in the brands, not in the products.

Consumer behavior is not as irrational as it might seem. Buying leading brands assures consumers of high-quality products without the need for constant testing and analysis. Life is short.

Better vs. first.

Which scenario seems more likely to you?

Scenario A: Company develops a better product or service that goes on to overtake an established market leader.

Scenario B: Company is first to launch a new brand in a new category and becomes the market leader, fending off dozens of competitors that try to take away its leadership by introducing better products or services.

Which scenario best describes brands like Starbucks, Red Bull, and iPod?

Or, going back a few years: Tide, Saran Wrap, Reynolds Wrap, Lipton, Nescafé, Intel, Jell-O, and dozens of other leader brands?

Scenario B fits the facts better. The first brand in a new category goes on to dominate that category over an extended period of time.

Scenario A fits the perceptions of the average left-brain logical thinker. And those perceptions are very strongly held.

It's the death-row dilemma. If you say you're innocent, we execute you because you show no remorse for your terrible crimes. If you say you're guilty, we execute you anyway, secure in the knowledge that we didn't send an innocent person to the gas chamber.

The better-product dilemma operates the same way. If you're first and become the market leader, you had the better product. If you're not first and didn't become the market leader, you didn't have the better product. Touché.

Some exceptions.

There are some categories in which the better product does win—categories with few or no brands. Notice, for example, how consumers will take their time to pick and choose the better apple, the better orange, or the better head of lettuce in the produce section of a supermarket.

The number of these "better-product-wins" categories keep declining because these are the best categories in which to launch new brands. In the produce section, a company called Fresh Express introduced the first brand of "packaged salad."

Naturally, the big produce companies jumped into the market with their big brand names: Dole and Del Monte, to name two.

So who's the market leader? Fresh Express, with some 40 percent of a $3 billion market.

In 2005, Fresh Express was bought by Chiquita Brands for $855 million, a nice bunch of green.

Think different and get rich. Think better and get frustrated.

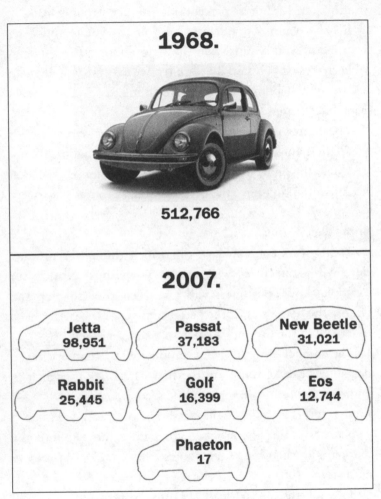

1968.

512,766

2007.

Jetta
98,951

Passat
37,183

New Beetle
31,021

Rabbit
25,445

Golf
16,399

Eos
12,744

Phaeton
17

In 1968, when it was focused on one vehicle,
Volkswagen sold 512,766 Beetles in America.
In 2007, even though it had seven models to sell,
Volkswagen sold just 221,760 vehicles.

CHAPTER 5

Management favors a full line.
Marketing favors a narrow line.

Logic favors the left-brain management approach. If you have a full line of products and services, you are obviously going to sell more products and services than if you have a narrow line.

So why do right-brain marketing people want a narrow line?

Because selling is the second step in a marketing program. The first step is building a brand in the mind. And with a full line that can be difficult.

What's a Chevrolet?

As of 2008, Chevrolet sold seven car models (Aveo, Cobalt, Corvette, HHR, Impala, Malibu, and Monte Carlo) and nine truck models (Avalanche, Colorado, Equinox, Express/G van, Silverado, Suburban, Tahoe, TrailBlazer, and Uplander).

When you sell everything under one brand name, it can be difficult for that one brand name to stand for anything.

Ask a car buyer, "What's a Chevrolet?" You're likely to get a long pause and a blank stare. Then maybe he or she will say, "It's an American car? Or truck?"

Management types tend to look at a market and ask themselves, "How do we carve out a decent share?" The obvious answer is the full line.

Management's next step is to turn to the marketing department and ask them to develop a strategy to promote the company's full line. The result is a meaningless slogan.

Chevrolet's current meaningless slogan: "An American Revolution."

Thank goodness, no one takes advertising slogans like this seriously. If they did, they might assume that under the front seat in every Chevrolet there's a secret compartment big enough to hold an AK-47.

You might be thinking that these are only words. What sells on the showroom floor is the quality of the product. That's partially true, too. But how do you get the prospect to walk the floor of a showroom?

What's a Ford?

Same problem as Chevrolet. As of 2008, Ford sold six car models (Crown Victoria, Five Hundred, Focus, Fusion, Mustang, and Taurus) and eleven truck models (E-series/ Club Wagon, E-series van, Edge, Escape, Escape Hybrid, Expedition, Explorer, F-series, Freestyle, Ranger, and Taurus X).

Unlike Chevrolet, Ford gave up trying to find a meaningless slogan that covers its entire range of models. Each Ford advertisement focused on one model with an iconic headline. Some examples:

- "Tough. Love." The 2008 Escape Hybrid.
- "MPGs meet MP3s." The new thirty-five-mile-per-gallon 2008 Focus.
- "Street Smart." The 2008 Edge with sync technology.
- "Safety. Fast." The 2008 Fusion.

Recently, however, Ford shifted gears and is trying out an omnibus slogan for the entire line. What brilliant idea will drive consumers into dealers' showrooms?

"Ford. Drive one."

Drive one? That's the difference between a Ford and the other thirty-five major automobile brands on the U.S. market? It's a childish idea that will never work.

Cars are not cola, a product category in which it's Coke and Pepsi and nobody else. The automobile field is intensely competitive. (There are twenty-nine brands that each sell more than a hundred thousand vehicles a year.)

Consumers don't need more choice on the showroom floor. They already have a full line of brands to choose from before they walk into a showroom.

Just like there are horses for courses, there are also strategies for categories. In an overcrowded category, there is only one strategy that will work. You need to oversimplify your marketing message.

But if you market everything under one brand name, how is this possible? Frankly, it isn't. That's why the U.S. automobile industry has been in terrible shape for such a long time.

"Look at all three."

That was the headline of a famous 1932 Plymouth advertisement. And readers instantly knew the names of the other two.

That was a year when Chevrolet, Ford, and Plymouth accounted for 65 percent of the automobile market.

"Look at all three" was an effective marketing approach. In 1932, Plymouth sales went up 19 percent, a year the total automobile market went down 43 percent.

Plymouth is gone, but what if Dodge, the low-end Chrysler brand, ran a similar ad today? Readers would be confused. Chevrolet, Ford, and Dodge account for only 33 percent of the automobile market.

Today, it takes seven brands to account for 65 percent of the automobile market.

Look at all seven? That doesn't make sense. Today the average car buyer is likely to visit only three dealer showrooms, generally of the same make, before doing the deal.

As time goes on, every category moves in the same direction. More brands, more choices, more confusion, more need for simplification.

Instead of adding to the confusion by model proliferation, car companies would be better off to simplify their offerings.

The sad saga of Saturn.

Launched in 1990, the Saturn automobile quickly became as famous as its namesake, the Saturn V12, the rocket that carried the Apollo astronauts to the moon.

In 1994, just four years after its introduction, Saturn hit its high-water mark, selling 286,003 cars. That year, the average Saturn dealer sold more vehicles than the average of any other brand.

- Saturn: 960 vehicles per dealer
- Toyota: 841 vehicles per dealer
- Ford: 746 vehicles per dealer
- Honda: 677 vehicles per dealer
- Nissan: 661 vehicles per dealer
- Chevrolet: 553 vehicles per dealer

Unlike the other major automobile brands, Saturn was available in one model only, although you could have the car in a two-door, a four-door, or a hatchback version.

That was the year the "Saturn spirit" was in full bloom. That was the year forty-four thousand owners and their families attended a "homecoming" at the Saturn plant in Spring Hill, Tennessee.

The following year, J.D. Power and Associates' annual sales satisfaction index ranked Saturn number one.

What did Saturn stand for in the minds of consumers? An inexpensive, good-looking compact car for young people.

What did Saturn do next?

Did Saturn management try to expand its share of the compact-car market? Or did Saturn management try to expand the line with larger and more-expensive vehicles?

What did every automotive "expert" tell Saturn it should do next? You're right. Expand the line.

A typical quote from that year: "Many analysts feel that Saturn will eventually need a bigger model to retain customers as they get older and more affluent," reported the *Wall Street Journal*.

In 1998, a General Motors vice president said, "We're doing everything we can to get them a wider product range."

That same year, an *Automotive News* editor wrote, "GM has to bite the bullet and let Saturn spread its wings. That is, give Saturn a full line of cars and light trucks as soon as practical."

The following year, Cynthia Trudell took over as head of Saturn, and, as you might expect, one of the first things she said was that Saturn is "definitely looking for ways to expand the portfolio."

Two years later, Ms. Trudell was gone and Annette Clayton took over. The strategy didn't change, however.

"My focus for the immediate future," said Ms. Clayton, "is to prepare us for the SUV launch and to position us to grow the portfolio."

The larger Saturn (the L series) was introduced in 1999. The sport-utility vehicle (the Vue) arrived in 2002, along with the Ion, a replacement for the original Saturn.

When Bob Lutz arrived at GM as vice chairman responsible for product development, he sounded the same tune. In 2004, he said, "We're investing in Saturn's future because the inherent health of the brand is quite good. It just needs a bigger, more exciting product portfolio."

Nothing helped. Saturn's sales fluctuated over the years, but never again reached its 1994 high-water mark of 960 vehicles per dealer.

In 2007, the average Saturn dealer (with five models to sell: Aura, Ion, Outlook, Sky, and Vue) sold only 553 vehicles.

When the management types got finished with Saturn, it wasn't an inexpensive car anymore because the larger, more-expensive models undermined that position.

When the management types got finished with Saturn, it wasn't for young people, either. As a matter of fact, the thinking behind the line-extension strategy was to "serve the customer" as he or she got older and wealthier.

After seventeen years, what did Saturn stand for?

Not much of anything.

What would marketing have done?

While the classic management approach is to expand the line, marketing generally has a different agenda.

The number one marketing objective is to dominate a category. When you do that, you are almost invulnerable to competitive threats. (Think Porsche in sports cars.)

In its high-water year, Saturn had 16 percent of the "small" or compact-car category. Out of twenty-three models of small cars, Saturn was second only to the Ford Escort.

- Ford Escort: 19 percent
- Saturn: 16 percent
- Honda Civic: 15 percent
- Toyota Corolla: 12 percent
- Chevrolet Cavalier: 11 percent
- Chevrolet/Geo Prizm: 7 percent
- All others: 15 percent

Sixteen percent is not exactly the lion's share of a category.

Instead of spending hundreds of millions of dollars developing larger, more-expensive Saturns, a marketing-oriented executive would have spent the money improving the basic model.

That way Saturn might be able to capture some of the 84 percent of the small-car market it didn't own. And build a dominant position in compact cars in much the same way that Volkswagen did in the 1950s and 1960s.

(Every high-tech product, from computers to automobiles, needs constant product development to keep pace with competition, much like a producer of calendars has to keep changing the year.)

It took Saturn eleven years to introduce an updated version of its S series, or small Saturn. In those same eleven years, Honda introduced three generations of its Civic compact.

In 1994, the Saturn S series outsold the Honda Civic by 7 percent.

In 2007, the Honda Civic outsold the S-series replacements (the Ion and the Aura combined) by 207 percent.

Compare Porsche with Volkswagen.

Today, Porsche dominates the sports-car category. In the past, Volkswagen dominated the compact-car category, but today the brand doesn't stand for much of anything.

The numbers demonstrate the difference. In 2006, Volkswagen had sales of $138.4 billion and net profits of $3.6 billion, or a net profit margin of just 2.6 percent.

Porsche, on the other hand, had sales of $10.2 billion in 2006, with net profits of $1.7 billion, or a net profit margin of an astounding 16.7 percent.

Almost every management guru says the automobile business is the world's most difficult business. But not if you produce a narrow line that stands for something in the minds of consumers.

With a net profit margin of 16.7 percent, Porsche ranks right up there with big money makers like Coca-Cola (20.7 percent), Procter & Gamble (13.5 percent), General Electric (12.9 percent), and IBM (10.5 percent).

Management wisdom dies hard.

When you believe in something, you seldom change your mind. When you believe in something, what you generally do when faced with facts that seem to contradict your beliefs is to fault the execution, not the strategy.

"Saturn didn't move fast enough to expand the brand" goes the thinking of the logical left-brain management crowd.

Yeah, sure.

STRONG & NATURAL.

Founder Dietrich Mateschitz recently announced
the introduction of Red Bull cola.
In three to five years, he predicted his cola sales
would equal his energy-drink sales. (Unlikely.)

CHAPTER 6

Management tries to expand the brand.
Marketing tries to contract the brand.

Man who chases two rabbits," Confucius once said,
"catches neither."

Obviously, Confucius was not management material,
because the number one goal of left-brain managers everywhere is "growth." And how do you grow? Logic suggests a
company needs to expand.

So instead of chasing one rabbit, a company starts chasing
two rabbits. Or maybe three rabbits.

Right-brain marketing people see things differently. In
order to grow in profits, if not in sales, companies need to
contract the brand, rather than expand it. That may not be
logical, but it works.

The clearest example of the difference between contraction
and expansion is the battle between Nokia and Motorola.

Nokia contracts.

In 1967, before Nokia saw the wisdom of contraction,
it went on an acquisition binge and merged with Finnish

Rubber Works, a rubber footwear and tire manufacturer, and Finnish Cable Works, a cable and electronics manufacturer. Then, in 1981, Nokia acquired a majority interest in a telecom company. The following year, Nokia acquired interests in Scandinavia's largest maker of color television sets and a Swedish electronics and computer firm. In 1986, Nokia acquired control of Finland's largest electrical wholesaler. In 1988, Nokia purchased Ericsson's IT division to create the largest information-technology group in Scandinavia.

This mindless expansion came to a screeching halt in the 1990s, as Nokia focused on cell phones and sold off everything else. Now Nokia was all set to chase one rabbit only.

In 1998, Nokia sold more than 40 million cell phones to surpass Motorola and become the world's No.1 cell-phone manufacturer, a position it has held ever since.

Meanwhile, Motorola was going in exactly the opposite direction.

Motorola expands.

The company started as a manufacturer of car radios, hence the name Motorola. Over the years, Motorola moved into a host of different businesses: pagers, semiconductors, television-set-top boxes, cable modems, home-theater equipment, automotive electronics, telecommunications gear.

Although Nokia became the leader in cell phones, Motorola was the company that had invented the product. In 1983, the company introduced the first commercially available mobile phone, the Motorola DynaTAC 8000X.

As the cell phone started to take off in the late 1980s, Motorola should have focused the entire company on its cell-phone product. Instead, Motorola continued to chase a number of rabbits.

In 1990, Motorola introduced a line of computer workstations. Also that year, Motorola organized the sixty-six-satellite Iridium communications system, which cost about $5 billion to construct and went online in 1998. (Two years later, Iridium was sold for $25 million.)

In 1991, Motorola began developing the PowerPC chip with Apple and IBM. It later introduced a line of Motorola personal computers using that same chip.

By 1995, Motorola was calling itself "One of the world's leading providers of wireless communications, semiconductors and advanced electronic systems, components and services. Major equipment businesses include cellular telephone, two way radio, paging and data communications, personal communications, automotive, defense and space electronics and computers."

(Read the preceding paragraph again. If you can't describe your brand in two or three words, you have a serious marketing problem.)

In 1997, Motorola announced it would build a second global satellite system for $12.9 billion.

In 2000, Motorola bought General Instruments in a deal valued at $17 billion. In the following years, the acquisitions continued with the purchase of a cable network equipment company, an embedded computing systems company, and a passive optical networking equipment maker.

It wasn't until 2004 that Motorola decided to slim down by spinning off its semiconductor operations. Since then, the company has divested a number of operations, culminating in its 2008 plan to spin off its crown jewel, the cell-phone division. (About twenty years too late.)

Look at the numbers.

It's not how many products you make that determine whether a company is successful or not; it's how much money you make.

- In the last ten years, Motorola had revenues of $329.3 billion and Nokia had revenues of $370.1 billion. The two were close in sales.
- In the last ten years, Motorola had a net income of $5.4 billion, or a net profit margin of 1.6 percent. Nokia had a net income of $44.0 billion, or a net profit margin of 11.9 percent, seven times as much as Motorola.
- On the stock market, Motorola is worth $9.0 billion. Nokia is worth $48.2 billion, more than five times as much as Motorola.
- According to Interbrand, Motorola is the eighty-seventh most valuable brand in the world, worth $3.7 billion. Nokia is the fifth most valuable brand, worth $35.9 billion, almost ten times as much as Motorola.
- In 2007, Nokia had 37.8 percent of the world's cell-phone market, while Motorola languished in third place with just 14.3 percent of the market.

Motorola expanded its brand, while Nokia contracted its brand. The big winner? Nokia, of course.

But that's not how Motorola management sees it. The new CEO, Gregory Brown, faults "inconsistent execution" in the cell-phone business for much of Motorola's troubles.

When things go bad, left brainers always blame the execution. How could a logical, analytical, meticulously developed strategy be at fault?

Rabbits in the sky.

Take the airline industry. Management often makes decisions that are right in the short term and wrong in the long term.

One of the first decisions most airlines had to make was "Should we carry passengers or cargo?"

"Let's chase both rabbits" was the unanimous reply. "We have extra space under the passenger compartments, so it's a no-brainer." So every major airline in the United States carries both passengers and cargo.

Not very much cargo, though. In 2007, American Airlines' cargo revenue was $825 million. That sounds like a lot, but it was only 4 percent of the airline's revenues.

(The urge to expand is universal. At one point in time, United Parcel Service had the dumb idea of putting seats on its planes on the weekends and flying charter passengers. And maybe changing its name to UPPS, United Parcel & Passenger Service?)

The next decision for the airline industry was passenger destinations. "Should we fly to business or vacation destinations?"

"Let's chase both rabbits" was the almost unanimous reply. "Why should we limit ourselves? Houston or Honolulu? We can do both."

The next decision was the scope of operations. "Should we fly domestic or international?"

"Let's chase both rabbits" was the almost unanimous reply. So every major U.S. airline flies passengers and cargo to both domestic and foreign cities.

The next decision was the class of service. "Should we offer first-class, business-class, or coach-class service?"

"Let's chase all three rabbits" was the almost unanimous reply. So every major airline has multiple classes of service.

(The rabbits keep multiplying. American Airlines now has eight classes of service: Economy Super Saver, Economy Saver, Economy Flexible, Instant Upgrade, Business Special, Business Flexible, First Flexible and First.)

In retrospect, it's easy to see the fallacy of a multiple-rabbit approach. But in the short term, many of these management moves did increase revenues and profits.

It's only in the long term, and in the presence of narrowly focused competition, that a multiple-rabbit strategy tends to fall apart.

Enter Southwest, the one-rabbit airline.

Business destinations only, no vacation destinations. Coach class only, no first- or business-class service. Domestic flights only, no international service.

Southwest narrowed its focus in many other ways. The airline serves no food, except peanuts. Doesn't carry pets. Doesn't allow advance-seating reservations or interairline baggage exchange. Doesn't give corporate discounts.

(Southwest recently announced a new category of "Business Select" fares that cost $10 to $30 more one way and provide preferential boarding, bonus frequent-flier credits, and a free cocktail. (Is this a hint of things to come? If so, not a good direction.)

As a result of its one-rabbit strategy, Southwest Airlines can operate its system with only one type of aircraft, the Boeing 737. Delta, for example, operates eight types of aircraft. So does American Airlines.

(Delta is merging with Northwest Airlines. After the merger, unless it sells some planes, Delta will be flying thirteen different types of airplanes.)

A narrow focus improves operations—one reason why Southwest consistently has the lowest complaint ratio in the industry. In 2007, complaints per one hundred thousand passengers were a fraction of those of the five largest U.S. airlines.

- Southwest: 0.26 complaints
- Northwest: 1.43 complaints
- American: 1.65 complaints
- Delta: 1.81 complaints
- United: 2.25 complaints
- US Airways: 3.16 complaints

A narrow focus improves maintenance. The entire maintenance and servicing operation is much easier to manage if your mechanics and scheduling staff are working with one type of aircraft.

(Maybe better maintenance had nothing to do with it, but in more than three decades of operations, Southwest Airlines has never had a passenger fatality. The only other major airline in the world that can match that record is Qantas.)

Meanwhile, back at the multiple-rabbit airlines.

- United went bankrupt.
- Delta went bankrupt.
- US Airways went bankrupt.
- Northwest went bankrupt.

And American Airlines, in the last ten years, has had revenues of $195.2 billion and managed to lose $4.3 billion.

The problems in the airline industry are only going to get worse. With the recent surge in fuel costs, you might think that America's multiple-rabbit airlines would give some thought to revamping their strategies.

But nothing has changed. They are meeting the threat posed by Southwest with their usual approach: chase everything that moves.

"Should we run a full-service airline or a no-frills airline?"

"Let's chase both rabbits." So Delta Air Lines launched Song, which it later folded. And United Airlines launched Ted, which it also later folded.

On the other hand, we believe there is an opportunity for an airline to use a marketing strategy that is the exact opposite of Southwest. Launch a one-rabbit, all-first-class airline, a strategy that was tried (unsuccessfully) by Eos and MaxJet on the North Atlantic route.

You need a certain amount of guile to be successful in business today. You don't attack the major airlines on their most profitable route, New York to London.

Southwest didn't start on the New York to Los Angeles route. Its first flights were from Dallas to Houston and San Antonio. It wasn't until eight years later that Southwest branched out of Texas to serve New Orleans, Oklahoma City, and Tulsa.

By the time the major airlines figured out what Southwest was up to, it was too late for them to do anything about it.

"The most-overpaid CEO in America."

That's the epitaph often applied to Robert Nardelli, former chief executive of Home Depot. After six years, he left the company with an exit package valued at about $210 million.

If you looked just at Home Depot's numbers, Nardelli did a good job. In six years, sales were up 99 percent and profits were up 125 percent.

But compare Home Depot to Lowe's, the number two home-improvement chain. When Nardelli took over, Home Depot had revenues that were 2.4 times that of Lowe's. When Nardelli left, Home Depot had revenues that were only 1.9 times that of Lowe's.

During that same time period, Home Depot stock lost 8 percent of its value, while the stock of Lowe's was up 188 percent.

There's still plenty of room for growth at both chains. Lowe's estimates the annual U.S. home-improvement market is $700 billion. If that's true, Home Depot and Lowe's combined have less than 20 percent of the market.

Dominant brands usually outperform their smaller rivals. McDonald's is growing faster than Burger King. Budweiser has Miller on the ropes. Gillette is outperforming Schick. Nike is way ahead of Reebok. Why did Home Depot fail to keep pace with its smaller rival?

Instead of staying focused on its consumer business, Home Depot spent more than $6 billion on acquisitions to bulk up

---

Home Depot Supply, its major effort to get into the building-supply business.

With only about 13 percent of the home-improvement market, Home Depot should have rigidly focused on its core business.

All growth is not alike. Growth in its home-improvement business strengthens the brand. Growth outside the core weakens the brand.

The grass is always greener on the other side of the fence. Why is it that a company like Home Depot keeps looking for other businesses to get into when it still hasn't dominated its existing business?

Furthermore, building supply and home supply are two different businesses. "Contractors rely on longstanding relationships with suppliers and trained salespeople," the *Wall Street Journal* pointed out. "Many associate The Home Depot brand with do-it-yourselfers and soccer moms pushing shopping carts, and avoid the stores."

Home Depot's approach is typical of companies that try to grow their businesses by (1) line extension, (2) diversification, and (3) synergy.

Right-brain marketing people know that none of these strategies can compare with the power of a simple focus.

"The most over-hyped CEO in America."

That's the epitaph often applied to Donald Trump, whose triumphs are trumpeted daily in the media.

Not everything has gone well for The Donald, though. In 2004, Trump Hotels & Casino Resorts announced that it would file for bankruptcy. Shareholders took a financial bath.

What went wrong? If you listen to The Donald, the Trump

brand is one of the strongest brands in the world. How could three Atlantic City casinos bearing his name wind up in the Chapter 11 Dumpster?

Management wisdom always focuses on operating errors. He paid too much when he bought the Taj Mahal; he didn't renovate his facilities fast enough to keep up with the competition; he didn't spend enough on advertising; he lost market share to the more luxurious Borgata Hotel Casino and Spa.

All of these errors probably played a role in his downfall, but what about his marketing strategy?

Seriously flawed, in our opinion. (Disclosure: Years ago, Al's advertising agency was on the receiving end of Trump's signature phrase, "You're fired.")

Al's agency worked for Holiday Inns, owners of Harrah's Marina in Atlantic City. The company wanted to build another casino in town, but on the Boardwalk instead of in the Marina area. So they struck a fifty-fifty deal with the Trump Organization.

The name they selected: Harrah's Boardwalk.

Wait a minute, Al said. That's a classic line-extension mistake. There are a certain number of loyal Harrah's customers, and now you are going to take that number and divide it by two. Half to Harrah's Marina and half to Harrah's Boardwalk.

Furthermore, "The Other Atlantic City," the marketing strategy for Harrah's Marina, emphasized the difference between the two locations.

Presumably, the Marina customer was more laid-back and refined than the Boardwalk customer. (One facetious ad headline considered, but not used: "At Harrah's Marina, the animals are in the show, not in the audience.")

After much discussion, both sides settled on the name Trump Plaza. The marketing strategy: "Atlantic City's Centerpiece," taking advantage of Trump Plaza's location in the middle of the Boardwalk and Donald Trump's reputation for building the biggest and the best.

Later, Holiday Inns sold its half of Trump Plaza to Donald Trump, who proceeded to make the same line-extension mistake that Al warned Holiday Inns about.

Eventually, Trump put his name on three Atlantic City casinos, dividing his loyal customers into thirds and practically guaranteeing the bankruptcy to come.

Why left brainers love line extension.

Because it's logical. If you have a good brand name, why can't you use that good brand name on everything?

Right-brain holistic thinkers recognize that line extension can work in the absence of strong competition (which is the case for the Trump condominiums in many cities around the world.)

But in the presence of strong competition, line extension is the road to disaster.

Apparently, there weren't any right-brain holistic thinkers around to tell Donald Trump not to put the Trump name on a second and a third Atlantic City casino.

Or if there were, they hesitated to speak up. We don't blame them. Disagreeing with The Donald is not a job for the faint of heart.

Creative Nomad Jukebox was a "first mover,"
the first high-capacity MP3 player on the market.
Apple's iPod was the "first minder,"
the first brand to get into consumers' minds.

CHAPTER 7

Management strives to be the "first mover."
Marketing strives to be the "first minder."

In management circles, one of the most talked-about concepts is the "first-mover" advantage.

Some management consultants swear by it. Others downplay the idea. Over the years, there have been many articles on the subject, both pro and con.

In marketing circles, the first-mover advantage is irrelevant. What matters is the "first-minder" advantage.

In a new category, the first brand that gets into consumers' minds is almost always the winner. Gatorade in sports drinks. Dr Pepper in spicy cola. Activia in probiotic yogurt.

Apple wasn't first with the iPod.

The iPod, an MP3 player with a hard-disk drive, was first sold in retail stores in the United States on November 11, 2001.

More than a year earlier (in July 2000), Creative Technology Ltd., a Singapore company, was selling the Creative Nomad Jukebox, an MP3 player with a hard drive, in the U.S. market.

Furthermore, the Creative Nomad Jukebox had a six-gigabyte hard drive versus only five gigabytes for the initial iPod.

The Creative Nomad Jukebox got into the market first, but not into the mind first. It didn't have a chance to get into the mind first because the company made four basic marketing mistakes.

1. *Line extension.* Creative Technology was already selling two other MP3 players, the Creative Nomad II and the Creative Nomad II MG (magnesium case).

Both of these products had sixty-four-megabyte flash-memory storage, which meant they could hold only about twenty songs instead of the thousands of songs that a hard drive could hold.

In other words, the hard-drive MP3 player was a totally separate category. Using the Creative name on both categories caused confusion, which undermined the brand-building process.

2. *A generic name.* "Creative" is a descriptive, generic name. You can't build a brand with a generic name. You need a brand name.

What's a brand name? It's a manufactured name like iPod, or a generic name used out of context. (Apple doesn't sell apples.) And there are a host of other marketing criteria to determine whether a given name would make a good brand name.

3. *A long, complicated name.* Compare "Creative Nomad Jukebox" (seven syllables) versus "iPod" (two syllables).

If you want to build a worldwide brand in today's overcrowded marketplace, you need a short, simple brand name.

(Brands like Red Bull, Starbucks, and Grey Goose also are two-syllable names.)

For a brand name to become truly successful, it needs to become the nickname for the category. Nobody calls the category "hard-disk-drive MP3 players." They call them "iPods," even the hard-disk-drive MP3 players made by other companies. (All pocket-tissue brands are often called "Kleenex.")

A first mover should always ask itself, "Does my name have a chance to become the generic name for the new category?"

4. *A lack of focus.* In addition to making MP3 players, Creative Technology made a host of other products: the Creative Zen Portable Media Center (another bad brand name), digital cameras, graphic accelerator cards, modems, CD and DVD drives, PC speakers, audio chips, and electronic musical instruments.

Creative management should have done what Nokia did. Drop everything in order to focus on a hot product, the hard-drive MP3 player.

(Creative did achieve a minor moral victory by collecting a $100 million technology-licensing fee from Apple.)

How do you create an iPod?

It's simple—and, at the same time, difficult. You become the first brand in a new category in the mind. No other strategy is as effective as this fundamental marketing law. Be first in the mind.

No other strategy can produce as much profitable sales over the long term. No other strategy is as easy to execute. No other strategy compares with the simple strategy of being "first in the mind."

- Coca-Cola, the world's most valuable brand, was the first cola.
- McDonald's, the world's largest fast-food company, was the first hamburger chain.
- Nescafé, the world's largest-selling coffee, was the first instant coffee.

It's a message left-brain management people don't want to hear. They think it downgrades the quality of their people and their organizations. They think it implies that knowledge, skill, and effort don't matter. That all you need to do to be successful is to be first.

Too many management people hear only the first half of the marketing message: the importance of being first. They don't hear the second half of the message: what right-brain marketing people mean by being first. Being first in the mind, not in the marketplace.

They confuse "first mover" with "first minder."

In our investigation of brands, we find that very few leading brands were ever literally first in the marketplace. Usually, there were a few misstarts before someone figured out how to get the brand into the consumer's mind.

- Duryea built the first automobile in America, but the brand never got into the mind. Ford was the first brand in the mind (and is still a leading automobile brand today.)
- Du Mont built the first television set in America, but the brand never got into the mind.
- Hurley built the first washing machine in America, but the brand never got into the mind.

When you look around the world, you find many brands like Duryea, Du Mont, and Hurley. First movers, but not first minders.

What could have been big winners turn out to be modest successes at best.

What's a Krating Daeng?

Outside of Thailand, few people know.

Krating Daeng is a lightly carbonated, highly caffeinated concoction containing liberal quantities of herbs, B-complex vitamins, and amino acids.

But it wasn't anyone in Thailand who took that concoction and built a worldwide brand. It was an Austrian named Dietrich Mateschitz who discovered the drink, saw its potential, and did a deal with the company.

A temptation that's hard to resist is to give a new idea an "exotic" name as Motorola did with the first cell phone, the Motorola DynaTAC 8000X, and MITS did with the first personal computer, the MITS Altair 8800. And Asus is doing with the first ultracompact laptop, the Asus Eee PC.

(Exotic names have a long history. The first match was called a "sulphuretted peroxide strikable." The first lie detector was called a "cardio-pneumo-psychograph.")

Mateschitz could have used the name Krating Daeng, for example. Or perhaps he could have called the new drink Thailand Tea.

What Mateschitz actually did was to call his Asian compound "an energy drink"—as it happens, the first energy drink. As a brand name, he picked Red Bull, a variation on the English translation of Krating Daeng: "red water buffalo."

Simple names work best when defining a new category and creating a new brand name. Not only is "energy drink" a simple name, it also benefits from an analogy with Power-Bar, the first "energy bar."

Right brainers are visually oriented. They think of marketing as "filling an empty hole in the mind." If there's a category called energy bar, the consumer thinks, there must also be a category called energy drink.

"Energy drink" works as a category name even though there is little relationship between the ingredients in a can of Red Bull and the ingredients in energy bars like PowerBar, Balance, Clif, and Luna.

Management people are often too logical when they try to figure out a name for a new category. What matters most is not describing the benefits of the new category but rather expressing the essence of the new category in as simple a way as possible.

Red Bull became a great brand because "energy drink" was perceived as something that improves a person's performance during times of increased stress or strain, which some people took to mean sexual performance. ("Energy" is just a way of expressing that idea in a socially acceptable way.)

Left brainers are verbally oriented. They think of marketing as communicating a laundry list of benefits.

How do you verbalize the benefits of consuming a caffeinated drink containing herbs, B-complex vitamins, and amino acids? It's easy to see why the big soft-drink companies ignored Krating Daeng.

Then, too, the soft-drink management people were busy trying to squeeze the last ounce of value out of their existing brands. That's why there are now fourteen different varieties of Coca-Cola.

Google wasn't first in search.

The last time we checked, Google was worth $91.6 billion on the stock market, more than fourteen times as much as General Motors and Ford combined.

Not bad for two Stanford University graduate students who started the company in 1998 (and never did get their PhD's.)

What made Google one of the world's most valuable brands, and in the process made some one thousand Google employees millionaires? It wasn't advertising.

In a recent year, Google spent just $5 million on marketing. (That same year, General Motors and Ford spent $5.9 billion on advertising in the United States alone.)

What made Google worth $91.6 billion? Round up the usual suspect—the better mousetrap. Google designed the better search engine.

Google is an interesting case history because it wasn't first and did become the market leader, apparently overturning all of our right-brain marketing concepts and proving once again that the better product wins in the marketplace.

We say "apparently" because the facts paint a different picture, providing left-brain management types with a plethora of ideas to think about.

The first search engine in the mind was AltaVista. But "search" wasn't good enough for AltaVista, so it added e-mail, directories, topic boards, comparison shopping, and loads of advertising on the home page.

It also spent more than a billion dollars to buy a number of companies, including Shopping.com, a comparison-shopping site, and Raging Bull, a financial site.

In essence, AltaVista turned itself into a portal. The site was later sold to CMGI, an Internet holding company, and eventually sold to Overture.

Overture was later sold to Yahoo! which restored AltaVista to its original vision as a search engine. But by then it was too late. Google had arrived.

The second search engine in the mind was GoTo.com, which actually invented the pay-per-click model. Then greed entered the picture and GoTo.com decided to syndicate its search service to MSN.com, Netscape, and AOL.

The syndication service was much more profitable than the destination site, so GoTo.com management decided to change its name to Overture and focus on its syndication service. (A good short-term decision, but a bad long-term one.)

When you have a choice between building a brand and building a business, it's always better to focus on the brand first. The business can follow.

The third search engine in the mind was Google, and the rest is history.

Thousands of left-brain management people literally let opportunities slip through their fingers because they fail to keep their brands focused.

It happened to AltaVista. It happened to GoTo.com. And it happened to many other companies that could have wound up winning the stock-market lottery.

Lexus wasn't the first Japanese luxury car.

Acura was. So why isn't Acura the leading luxury-car brand?

To understand marketing, you have to study history. The first Acura was sold in America in March 1986. The first Lexus wasn't sold until September 1989, three and a half years later.

The first Infiniti wasn't sold until December 1989.

Acura started like gangbusters. In its first full year (1987), it became the best-selling luxury import, outselling Volvo, Mercedes-Benz, BMW, Audi, and Jaguar. It was also ranked number one in customer satisfaction by J.D. Power and Associates.

So you might expect the sales order of Japanese luxury-car brands today to be (1) Acura, (2) Lexus, and (3) Infiniti. But it was Lexus, not Acura, that won this particular battle.

What happened to Acura? Like AltaVista and GoTo.com, Acura didn't have the courage of its convictions. It wasn't a "pure" luxury car.

The year Lexus was introduced, Acura was selling two models: the four-cylinder Integra, with a list price of $11,950 to $15,950; and the six-cylinder Legend, with a list price of $22,600 to $30,690.

Lexus also was selling two models, but they were six- and eight-cylinder cars: the ES 250, with a list price of $21,050; and the LS 400, with a list price of $36,000.

Lexus cars were more luxurious, with bigger, more powerful engines. They cost, on average, 40 percent more than Acura cars.

As Starbucks, Grey Goose, Häagen-Dazs, Evian, and a host of other high-end brands have demonstrated, you need a high price to build a luxury brand. Cheap is the enemy of chic.

Rome wasn't ruined in a day, either. In spite of its flawed strategy, Acura held its high-end leadership for twelve straight years. It wasn't until 1999 that Lexus finally passed Acura to become the leading Japanese luxury-car brand.

(During the decade of the 1990s, we wonder how many Lexus executives were asking Toyota management for less-expensive four-cylinder cars in order to compete more effectively with Acura.)

Today, Lexus is the largest-selling luxury-vehicle brand in the United States. In 2007, for example, Lexus was head and shoulders above all the others in units sold.

Lexus: 329,177
BMW: 293,795
Mercedes-Benz: 253,277
Cadillac: 214,726
Acura: 180,104
Lincoln: 131,487
Infiniti: 127,038

Left-brain managers are often decisive leaders who set clear-cut goals and demand rapid results.

Right-brain marketers often have patience. It can take a long time to change minds. Marketing itself can be described as "psychology in practice." (Witness the decades some people spend with their therapists.)

As Lexus demonstrates, companies need patience as much as they need gung-ho leadership. If you can't be first, then you can often be successful by keeping your focus while your competitors are losing theirs.

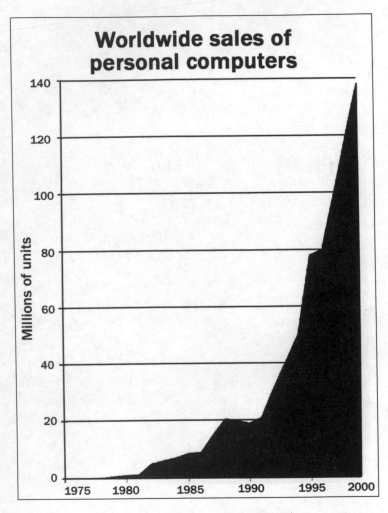

Worldwide sales of
personal computers

Millions of units

140

120

100

80

60

40

20

0

1975   1980   1985   1990   1995   2000

The twentieth century's most important product,
the PC took 25 years to reach its potential.
You can't accelerate the process
with massive marketing expenditures.

CHAPTER 8

Management expects a "big-bang" launch. Marketing expects a slow takeoff.

Among left-brain management folks, one of the enduring myths is that a new brand has to take off in a hurry . . . if it's eventually going to become a big brand.

Therefore, a company should devote enormous resources to a "big-bang" introduction.

Not true.

Right-brain marketing people intuitively know that the more revolutionary the concept, the longer it is going to take to gain acceptance.

Trivial products or ideas might take off rapidly, but not products that end up changing the way we live or work.

The slow growth of the personal computer.

The first PC was introduced in 1975, the same year Bill Gates dropped out of Harvard to go to Albuquerque, New Mexico, to write a basic software program for the MITS Altair 8800 computer.

Microsoft, the company Gates founded, is today one of

the most valuable companies in the world, worth $180.6 billion on the stock market.

Things weren't always so rosy. On February 3, 1976, Bill Gates wrote an open letter to Altair users complaining about software piracy. Published in the Homebrew Computer Club newsletter, Gates stated, "The amount of royalties we have received from sales to hobbyists makes the time spent on Altair BASIC worth less than $2 an hour."

Most people who found themselves toiling for less than two bucks an hour would have looked for some other line of work. Not Bill Gates. His faith in the future of his software paid off in a big way.

But the personal-computer category itself took off rather slowly. Here is one estimate of worldwide PC sales every five years since its introduction.

1975: 2,000
1980: 1,050,000
1985: 7,100,000
1990: 20,000,000
1995: 50,000,000
2000: 138,000,000

Around the turn of the century, personal-computer sales began to level off. In other words, it took twenty-five years for the PC to get into orbit as the market slowly changed from a nerd market to a business market to an everybody market.

Not exactly a rocket-ship launch.

The slow takeoff of a revolutionary product can convince management types that the market is going to be small. As

Ken Olsen, founder of Digital Equipment, famously said in 1977, "There is no reason for any individual to have a computer in his home."

The slow growth of the iPod.

Perhaps the most successful new product of the twenty-first century is Apple's iPod. Most people probably think the iPod took off in a big hurry.

It's true that the length of time from introduction to maturity is short by consumer product standards, but the iPod's year-to-year numbers show the same slow growth pattern of all serious products.

Here are iPod sales for the product's first six (fiscal) years.

2002: 345,000
2003: 1,306,000
2004: 4,540,000
2005: 22,497,000
2006: 39,409,000
2007: 51,630,000

As a glittering generality, new products that take off in a hurry turn into fads. Compare serious products like the iPod and the PC with a trivial product like the hula hoop, introduced in 1958.

In the first two years, Wham-O sold 100 million hula hoops. A few years later, the fad was over. Bartles & James, Clearly Canadian, Smirnoff Ice, Cabbage Patch Dolls, and many other brands have followed this trajectory.

The revolution that never happened.

When Kimberly-Clark introduced Cottonelle Fresh Roll-wipes in January 2001, the company thought it had another Kleenex on its hands: "America's first and only disposable, premoistened wipe on a roll."

The result of $100 million in research and backed by thirty patents, the new product, according to the corporation's press release, "is the most significant category innovation since toilet paper first appeared in roll form in 1890."

Maybe so.

But Kimberly-Clark introduced the product as if it were another hula hoop. The first year's advertising budget was $35 million. Expected first-year sales: $150 million. (First-year sales of the personal computer were less than $1 million.)

Within six years, Kimberly-Clark predicted sales of $500 million a year.

It never happened. Today, eight years later, Cottonelle Fresh Rollwipes is still a small struggling brand but finally showing some signs of life.

Left-brain managers focus on the numbers: the expected sides of $150 million the first year. Right-brain marketers would have focused on the problem of selling the idea.

"Wet toilet paper is a revolutionary concept. It's going to take a long time to get that idea off the ground and into the toilet." (If Kimberly-Clark had studied its own history, it would have found that its Kleenex brand didn't take off rapidly either.)

Forget advertising to reach everybody. When you want to change a fundamental human habit, you need to start with PR, or public relations.

Kimberly-Clark should also have heavily sampled the product, perhaps in high-end restaurants and hotels.

It was nerds who got the personal computer going. Cottonelle Fresh Rollwipes needed a similar group of people to serve as cadre for the wet-toilet-paper movement.

That's why the PR should have concentrated on a narrow segment of the market. Early adopters like to think they are starting a trend.

The line-extension name was also a major mistake. Cottonelle Fresh Rollwipes needed a shorter, more-distinctive brand name. (Maybe something like tPod.)

Theory A vs. Theory B.

Theory A (for airplane) is the airplane launch. Your new brand rolls slowly down the runway for thousands of feet and then, after a massive effort, slowly lifts off the tarmac. After your brand is airborne for a while, it starts to accelerate into its cruising altitude.

Theory B (for big bang) is the rocket-ship launch. Your new brand takes off like a rocket and then coasts into orbit.

Should you use massive advertising to launch a new brand? Or should you just use PR?

Advertising and its management supporters favor the rocket-ship launch because ad programs are traditionally launched with a big bang. And management wants its new product to take off in a hurry.

PR has no choice. It has to use an airplane launch. PR programs are invariably rolled out over an extended period of time. That's the only way PR can deal with the needs of media people who search for scoops and exclusives.

(You can't call up the media and say, "Everybody run my story on Monday. I'm launching my new brand with a big bang." That's not the way the media works.)

What about the real world? Do new brands take off like a rocket ship? Or do they take off like an airplane?

Take a typical new beverage brand. Here are annual sales of this new brand for the first five years (in euros).

1987: 800,000
1988: 1,600,000
1989: 2,800,000
1990: 5,200,000
1991: 11,600,000

The brand is Red Bull, a brand built primarily by PR, and one that took off slowly like an airplane.

No wonder management at Coca-Cola and the rest of the beverage industry ignored Red Bull. After five years on the market, annual sales, at the 1991 rate of exchange, were only $10 million.

It wasn't until 1999 (twelve years after the launch of Red Bull) that Coca-Cola got around to launching an energy drink called KMX. The product, of course, went nowhere.

If management waits to see if a new category develops into a big market, it's going to be too late to latch onto a decent market share.

Big companies take off slowly, too.

Take Microsoft. It might be hard to believe, but the brand took even longer to get off the runway than Red Bull.

It took Red Bull nine years to exceed $100 million in annual sales. It took Microsoft ten years to exceed $100 million in annual sales.

Take a third example. This retail brand took fourteen years to break $100 million in annual sales. Today, the brand does $339 billion in annual sales and has become the world's largest retailer.

The brand, of course, is Wal-Mart.

Maybe advertising agencies, PR agencies, consulting firms, and other marketing companies should take a tip from the medical profession.

Instead of calling their customers "clients," perhaps they should call their customers "patients."

Maybe then they wouldn't expect instant results.

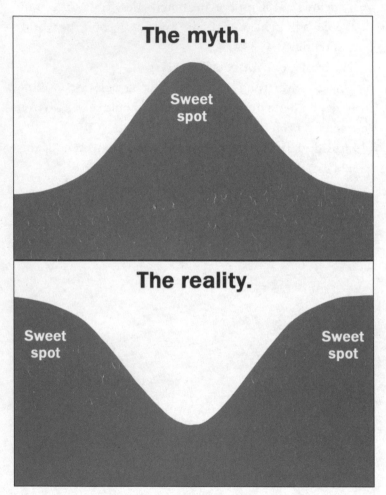

A market's center is not the best place to be.
The reality is that every category
tends to diverge into two separate categories,
one at the low end and one at the high end.

CHAPTER 9

Management targets the center of the market.
Marketing targets one of the ends.

Left-brain management types are highly analytical. If you want to build a big company, if you want to build a big brand, then you need to target your products and services to the heart, the "sweet spot," the center of the market.

That makes a lot of sense.

Right-brain marketing types know better. In every industry, the place to avoid is the mushy middle.

What industries are in trouble in America? The automobile industry, the department-store industry, and the airline industry. All three industries are in trouble for exactly the same reason.

The major companies in these industries target the center of the market.

The automobile industry.

The three major American companies (General Motors, Ford, and Chrysler) have been losing money.

All three companies have no strong low-end brands and no strong high-end brands.

At the low end, three imported brands—Hyundai, Kia, and Mazda—are doing great. As a matter of fact, Hyundai outsells every General Motors brand except Chevrolet. Here are 2007 vehicle sales in the U.S. market.

Hyundai: 467,009
Pontiac: 358,022
Kia: 305,473
Mazda: 296,110
Saturn: 240,091
Cadillac: 214,726
Buick: 185,791

At the high end, three imported brands—Lexus, BMW, and Mercedes-Benz—are also doing great. Here are 2007 vehicles sales in the U.S. market.

Lexus: 329,177
BMW: 293,795
Mercedes-Benz: 253,277
Cadillac: 214,726
Lincoln: 131,487

The American brands are strong in the middle and weak at the ends. And their problems are going to get worse. Why?

Every industry tends to diverge into two separate industries, one at the high end and one at the low end. But if you want to take advantage of this trend, you need to get in early and build your brand.

You can't wait until the market develops and then jump in. By then, it's too late.

The department-store industry.

Years ago, Sears, Roebuck and Company was the gold standard in the industry. Sears was the biggest, most profitable retailer in America.

No longer. Today, the 122-year-old company is in deep trouble.

In spite of a 2005 merger with Kmart and in spite of intensive efforts by Edward Lampert and his hedge fund, ESL Investments, sales are down. Recently, Sears Holdings Corp. announced plans to reorganize into several separate companies in order to pull the ailing retailer out of the doldrums.

What did Sears do wrong?

Nothing.

They just stayed in the middle of the market while the department-store industry was diverging into two separate industries, one at the low end and one at the high end.

At the low end, Wal-Mart and Target have become big moneymakers. Target has almost twice the revenues of Sears, and Wal-Mart has more than ten times the revenues. In 2007, Sears did $33.4 billion in sales, while Target did $63.4 billion and Wal-Mart did an incredible $339.0 billion.

At the high end, retailers like Nordstrom and Saks Fifth Avenue are doing well, as are a host of high-end boutiques.

Notice that the high end and the low end don't necessarily appeal to different consumers. As one pundit said, "Sometimes you want to go classy and sometimes you want to go slashy."

What should Sears have done? Logical left-brain managers

might have suggested that Sears, Roebuck follow the market by moving either upscale or downscale. But that's not good marketing logic.

Once you have a strong position in the mind, you can't change it. When you get into trouble, the answer to your problem is always the same: narrow the focus.

Sears should have narrowed its focus and become a specialist.

Sears was once America's leading seller of major appliances, with 41 percent of the market. That share is steadily eroding as Lowe's and Home Depot take appliance business away from them.

Instead of advancing to weakness (in clothing and soft goods) by buying Lands End for $1.9 billion, Sears should have been retreating to its strength in hard goods. Sears already owns a number of famous hard-goods brands like Kenmore, Craftsman, and DieHard.

But logical, growth-oriented management types would never think of that. It's always "expand, expand, expand."

The airline industry.

Airline management apparently likes the notion of appealing to the mass market because that way it can maximize market share. At least that's the theory.

Marketing people take a different point of view. Appealing to everybody is the ultimate in mushiness.

How successful would a restaurant be if it had a first-class section, a business-class section, and an economy section with separate menus and staffs?

How would you position that restaurant in a prospect's mind? Upscale, downscale, or somewhere in the middle?

A flying restaurant is no different.

At the low end, Southwest Airlines is doing well. So are other no-frills airlines like Ryanair in Europe, AirAsia in Asia, and Gol Airline in South America.

At the high end, the private-jet market is soaring. Furthermore, there is a stirring of interest in business-class-only service on a number of routes.

In the long run, we expect some high-end airline brands will emerge. It just makes good marketing sense.

Mushy thinking in the cola category.

Both Coca-Cola and Pepsi-Cola tried to introduce mid-calorie colas. Pepsi's product was called Pepsi Edge. Coca-Cola product was called C2.

With about 75 calories per twelve-ounce can, both products had roughly half the 150 calories found in a regular can of cola. According to Pepsi-Cola, its half-and-half product provides "the perfect balance of taste and calories."

From a marketing point of view, the new products were far from perfect. Pepsi drinkers who want "taste" will continue to drink regular Pepsi. Those who want "low calories" will continue to drink Diet Pepsi. Where's the market for Pepsi Edge?

Pepsi Edge doesn't win on "taste" and it doesn't win on "low calories." It's a classic mushy–middle management mistake.

The same holds true for C2.

Pepsi claims there are 60 million consumers who alternate between diet colas and regular colas. Maybe so, but there are also millions of consumers who alternate between coffee and tea, but that doesn't mean a product called "coftea" would be a big success.

This is the second time Pepsi-Cola made the same left-brain management mistake. Once before it tried a mid-calorie cola that never went anywhere. Launched in 1975, the product was called Pepsi Light.

Management is never one for admitting mistakes. Back in those days the company claimed that Pepsi Light was "ahead of its time." One could make the same claim today about Pepsi Edge. And they would be equally mistaken.

More mushy–middle management mistakes.

Red wine is a big seller. White wine is a big seller. But rosé wine is nowhere. Just because millions of wine drinkers alternate between red wine and white wine doesn't mean rosé can become a big seller.

Ketchup is a big seller in America. But so is salsa. As a matter of fact, a few years ago salsa overtook ketchup in sales. So what did Heinz do?

They introduced Heinz salsa-style ketchup. Another mushy–middle management mistake.

The best-selling brand of regular coffee in America is Folgers. So is the best-selling brand of decaf coffee. So Folgers saw an opportunity to plug a hole in the middle.

The result: Folgers 1/2 Caff. "Classic roast with half the caffeine." Another mushy-middle mistake that's unlikely to muster much market share.

The best-selling brand of regular cigarettes is Marlboro. So is the best-selling brand of "light" cigarettes. So Marlboro saw an opportunity in the middle.

The result: Marlboro Medium. (Cowboys are unlikely to smoke anything called "Medium.")

Expensive razor blades like Mach3 and Fusion are big sellers. So are disposables at the low end like Bic and Gillette. It's the razors in the middle that find their shares declining.

In digital cameras, the market has divided into (1) small-and-simple point-and-shoot cameras weighing six ounces or so, and (2) big-and-serious single-lens-reflex cameras weighing several pounds. There's just no market in the middle.

In watches, there's a big market for fashion watches like Swatch at the low end and prestige watches like Rolex at the high end. There just isn't much of a market in the mushy middle.

Then there's The Gap. After years of declining sales and failed turnaround attempts, the nation's largest specialty-apparel retailer is exploring a possible sale of the company or a spin-off of one or more of its three major brands: The Gap, Old Navy, and Banana Republic.

What went wrong at The Gap? From a marketing point of view, it was the 1994 launch of the Old Navy chain that now accounts for 43 percent of the company's revenues.

Old Navy is a no-frills, low-price clothing chain. A great concept, but the company already had a no-frills, low-price clothing chain called The Gap.

To make room for Old Navy, The Gap moved upscale right into the mushy middle, where it has had problems ever since.

(This is the same mistake General Motors made with Saturn and Chevrolet.)

How many items should a retailer stock?

A mass merchandiser like Wal-Mart stocks one hundred fifty thousand or so items and is very successful.

A warehouse club like Costco stocks about four thousand items and is also very successful. In its 2007 fiscal year,

Costco did $64.4 billion in sales.

In Europe, Aldi (short for Albrecht Discounts) stocks only thirteen hundred popular food items in its no-frills stores, but does about $45 billion in annual sales. (In Germany alone, Aldi has about 40 percent of the grocery market.)

Aldi is moving into the U.S. market where it now has 950 stores that generated $5.8 billion in sales in 2007.

How many items should a retailer stock? It all depends, but it's probably best to be at either the high end or the low end.

A logical left brainer might assume that there's always one way, the best way, to do anything.

An intuitive right brainer assumes there are two ways to do anything. And a third way, right in the mushy middle, that one should avoid at all costs.

Take the three mass merchandisers. Wal-Mart focused on low prices, so Target went slightly upmarket with wide aisles, neat displays, and designer merchandise.

Kmart tried to have low prices like Wal-Mart and designer merchandise (Martha Stewart, Joe Boxer, and others) like Target. Kmart went bankrupt.

In the early days of an emerging industry, you see repeated examples of the same folly. Companies jump in to provide the missing link between yesterday and tomorrow. Between cheap and expensive. Between fashionable and durable. Between hip and mainstream. Between young and old. Between tasty and diet.

Their motto: The best of both worlds.

Warning: The best of both worlds usually winds up in the mushy middle.

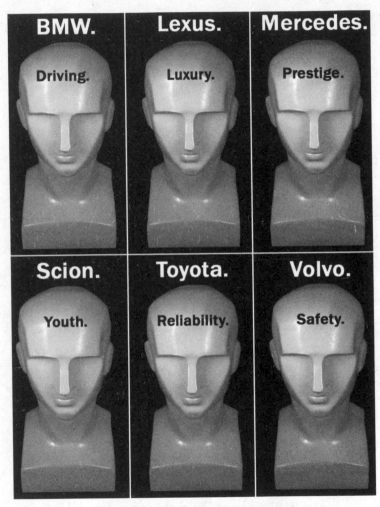

Many brands try to be all things to everybody,
a management approach that seldom works.
Most of the successful automobile brands
are focused on a single word or concept.

CHAPTER 10

Management would like to own everything.
Marketing would like to own a word.

A Hilton senior vice president was asked by a reporter,
"So what the hell is a Hilton?"

"People can't necessarily articulate it," conceded the
Hilton vice president. The brand is defined, he suggested,
"if we collectively give people an experience that says, yes,
I'm proud of what it says about me to stay here, it makes
me feel good; I'm in charge of my stay."

"I'm proud of what it says about me to stay here?" That's
a Hilton? That's what differentiates a Hilton from a Hyatt,
a Marriott, an Omni, a Radisson, a Ramada, a Sheraton, a
Westin, or a Wyndham?

Left-brain analytical types think, "Let's not get locked
into a single word or concept, but let's give the consumer a
good experience and he or she will be proud to return again
and again."

Delivering a good experience isn't enough.

Right-brain marketers want to supply a single word that sums up that experience. Otherwise, there's no way for a consumer to file the brand into the mind.

A prospect takes a test-drive in a BMW and hopefully he or she will say, "Wow, that's a great driving machine."

What's the role and function of marketing anyway? To collectively give people an experience that makes them proud of what it says about them? That's the role and function of the hotel itself. That's the role of left-brain management.

Sure, you want your product to give people a good experience. Without that, most marketing programs are certain to fail. But beyond a good experience is the need to position the brand.

What's a Hilton? The role of a marketing program is to answer that question, hopefully in a single word.

Times have changed. The objective of a marketing program used to be to make the brand famous. And years ago, when there were fewer brands and less advertising, that strategy worked well. Consumers tended to prefer the "well-known" brand in every category to the lesser-known brands.

Campbell's in soup. Morton's in salt. Listerine in mouthwash.

But today, with an avalanche of advertising, there are many well-known brands in every category. Take toothpaste, for example. Colgate, Crest, Aquafresh, Arm & Hammer, Mentadent, Sensodyne, Rembrandt, Close Up, Ultra Brite, and Pepsodent. Each of these brands is relatively well known.

What brand does a consumer buy?

The brand that owns a "position" in the mind. Aquafresh for "fresh breath." Close Up, a second choice for "fresh breath." Arm & Hammer for "baking soda." Mentadent for "baking soda/peroxide." Sensodyne for "sensitive teeth." Rembrandt for "high-end" toothpaste. Ultra Brite for "whiter teeth." And Pepsodent for the older crowd who remember when it was one of the best-selling toothpaste brands.

What about the two leading brands, Colgate and Crest? Not only are Colgate and Crest exceptionally well known but the two brands are perceived as the "leaders" in the toothpaste category.

Leadership alone is the best position your brand can own in the mind. When your brand is perceived to be the leader, consumers believe it is the best product or service. Not necessarily true, but that's the perception.

By the 1960s, Hilton was the best-known name in the hotel business. That was the perfect time to claim leadership in the hotel industry by answering the most important question in marketing: "What's a Hilton?"

Here it is forty years later, and Hilton still can't give a decent answer to that fundamental question.

Great brands are built by owning a word or concept in the mind.

- What's a Propel? Fitness water.
- What's a Domino's Pizza? Home delivery.
- What's a Tropicana? Not from concentrate.
- What's a Dyson? Never loses suction.
- What's a Quiznos? Toasted submarine sandwiches.
- What's a Popeyes? Spicy chicken.

What's a Kellogg?

Every year, *BusinessWeek* publishes its rankings of the top business schools in the country. The leaders bounce up and down, but five schools are consistently at the top of the list: (1) Northwestern's Kellogg, (2) Chicago, (3) Pennsylvania's Wharton, (4) Stanford, and (5) Harvard.

What does the average knowledgeable person associate with each of these five business schools? Ask, and we think you'll get the following answers.

- Kellogg: marketing
- Chicago: economics
- Wharton: finance
- Stanford: high technology
- Harvard: management

But of course. What's new about that?

What's new about that is that none of these business schools specialize in their specialties. Harvard is just as much a marketing school as Kellogg, and Kellogg is just as much a management school as Harvard. All teach a full range of business courses.

Then how did Kellogg get associated with marketing, an association that helped propel them to the top of the business-school list?

It was a fortuitous accident. On the faculty at Kellogg were a handful of nationally recognized marketing professors, most notably Phil Kotler.

To achieve success today, you have to get into minds. And to get into a mind, your prospect needs a place in his or her mind to put your brand.

The average business-school prospect starts out with nothing but empty slots in his or her mind for the names of business schools. Why would anyone try to remember the name of a business school unless he or she associates the school with an attribute, a location, or some other identifying concept?

So business-school prospects actively look for clues that will help them file the names of desirable schools. One or two mentions of Kotler and his achievements and *bang*, Northwestern's Kellogg is a marketing school.

On the other hand, there are a handful of business schools that have marketed themselves quite successfully by intentionally focusing on a single word or concept. Thunderbird (international studies) and Babson (entrepreneurs) are two.

People need help in sorting out names and concepts. Look at the vast number of lists of one thing or another: the *Fortune* 500, the *Inc* 500, the *Forbes* 400, the *New York Times* Best Sellers, the Interbrand 100, David Letterman's Top Ten, the *Billboard* music charts.

All of these various lists play into the need for people to have a simple way to file names and ideas in their minds.

What's a Volvo?

After the success of Volkswagen in the fifties and sixties, a host of imported European cars invaded the American market. Among them: English Ford, Fiat, Hilman, Opel, Peugeot, Renault, Simca, Triumph, Vauxhall, and Volvo.

Except for Volvo, none of these brands are still on the market.

What's a Volvo? A safe car. But none of these other brands managed to stand for anything in the car-buyer's mind.

What's worse, they didn't even try. The commonsense wisdom of the left-brain management crowd is that an expensive purchase like an automobile needs the support of a wide range of benefits: driving, comfort, style, power, reliability, low maintenance, low fuel consumption, low depreciation, and so on.

There's logic in this assumption, but the problem is in the execution. How are you going to put all these ideas into the consumer's mind? A company is lucky if it is able to associate one word or concept with its brand.

Volvo was lucky. Thanks to its invention of the three-point lap-and-shoulder seat belt and other safety features, Volvo is widely perceived to be the safe car.

For a number of years, Volvo was the largest-selling European luxury car in the American market, outselling Mercedes-Benz, BMW, Jaguar, and other brands.

Then Volvo started to back away from safety, introducing sports cars and convertibles. Its advertising started to talk about performance and other features. One top Volvo executive said recently, "Safety on its own is not enough."

In 1992, Volvo was the leading European luxury-car brand, selling 67,916 vehicles in the U.S. market. BMW sold 65,691 and Mercedes-Benz sold 63,312.

Today, BMW and Mercedes have left Volvo in the dust. Both brands sell way more than twice as many vehicles as Volvo does.

To an analytical management mind, no car buyer would buy a vehicle just because it's safe. But thanks to the halo effect, consumers think differently. If Volvo knows how to build safe cars, they probably know how to build reliable, fuel-efficient, dependable, durable cars, too.

To a holistic marketing mind, one thing (safety) leads to another.

What's a Lenovo?

The Chinese brand with the most global potential is Lenovo, the country's largest personal-computer maker. Formerly known as Legend Group Limited, the company bought IBM's PC operations in 2005 for $1.75 billion.

In addition to desktop and notebook PCs, Lenovo makes displays and storage drives, as well as a line of workstations. The company also has an IT services business.

Currently, Lenovo is tied with Acer, the Taiwanese company, as the world's third-largest PC manufacturer with a market share of 6.7 percent. (Hewlett-Packard leads with 19.1 percent. Dell is second with 15.2 percent.)

How can Lenovo move up the PC ladder? Here are three steps that a marketing person would likely take (and three steps that a management person would likely veto.)

1. *Focus the product line.* Leaders can sometimes get away with marketing a broad line of products and services, especially if they have a strong brand name like General Electric or Hewlett-Packard.

But is Lenovo a strong brand name? Not outside of China.

What should Lenovo focus on? That's a decision that should be easy to make. Recently, laptop and notebook computers have been outselling desktop computers. Furthermore, there's reason to believe desktop computers might someday become obsolete.

Lenovo should drop its desktop machines and focus on

notebook computers.

2. *Focus the company name.* Legend was a bad name; Lenovo is an even worse name. Sounds like an Italian dessert.

Fortunately in its IBM purchase, Lenovo was given a priceless present: the ThinkPad name that IBM used on its notebook computers.

Lenovo should change its name to ThinkPad Corporation.

ThinkPad is a unique and different name. Furthermore, it communicates the "notebook" idea, the new focus of the company.

3. *Focus on an attribute of the brand.* To build a brand, you need to stand for something in the prospect's mind. What should ThinkPad stand for?

As compared with a desktop machine, what's the weakness of a notebook computer? Battery life.

A desktop stays plugged in twenty-four hours a day. A notebook is limited to two or three hours of operation before needing a battery charge.

We would redesign the entire ThinkPad line in order to double or triple battery life, even if it meant selling heavier machines. (Every benefit comes with baggage.)

Furthermore, as batteries get better, that disadvantage would disappear.

Hopefully, the new ThinkPad Corporation could produce notebook computers that would run all day on a single charge.

That would mean a company employee could use his or her notebook computer all day long without recharging it. At the end of the day, the employee could plug the machine into an outlet so it would be ready to go again the next morning.

Slogan: "ThinkPad: the all-day notebook."

Dell just introduced the Latitude E6400 with a claimed battery life of "up to 19 hours," so an all-day notebook would be easy to produce.

There's a big difference, however, between marketing one all-day model like Dell is doing and having an entire line of all-day models that we think Lenoro should be doing. It's the same as the difference in the early days between Emery Air Freight and Federal Express.

Lenovo is currently successful because it can build computers in China very cheaply. But as the Chinese economy improves, as wages go up, that advantage will disappear.

While it lasts, Lenovo has an opportunity to build a worldwide brand that stands for something unique and different.

What's a Wal-Mart?

A few years ago, the CEO of Wal-Mart's advertising agency was asked, "What would you say is Wal-Mart's USP?"

Without hesitation, the agency CEO replied, "Value, loyalty, and quality."

(That answer would have appalled Rosser Reeves, the inventor of the Unique Selling Proposition concept.)

Value, loyalty, and quality? Those are words you might find hand-lettered on a mom-and-pop retail store in any small town in America.

On the outside of every Wal-Mart store are the words "We sell for less." In every Wal-Mart advertisement are the words "Always the low price. Always."

What word does Wal-Mart own in the mind? It's not *value, loyalty,* or *quality*. It's *cheap*. Not a bad word to own, either. It has made Wal-Mart the world's largest retailer.

Does *cheap* appeal to everybody? No, that's why *cheap* is a good word to own. Any combination of words that appeals to everybody will never work in marketing.

Value, loyalty, and quality? Who could ask for anything more?

As you probably know, Wal-Mart has a new slogan: "Save money. Live better." Once again, a great marketing slogan ("Always the low price. Always.") gets replaced by a platitude.

Look at a Hilton sibling, Hilton Garden Inn. What's a Hilton Garden Inn? According to the chain's advertising slogan, it's: "Everything. Right where you need it."

When you claim "everything," you end up with nothing.

On the other hand, an "everything" claim can sound exciting. Having worked for a number of advertising agencies, we know that exciting ideas are a lot easier to sell to management than simple positioning ideas.

What's an Embassy Suites?

In 1983, we were working for Holiday Inns when our client decided to get into the all-suite hotel business. The brand name they chose: Embassy Suites.

At the time, there were only two significant players in the all-suite category: Granada Royale, with twenty locations primarily in the western states; and Guest Quarters, with eight locations primarily in the East.

We were asked to make a presentation to Embassy Suites management. We made two points.

1. The first brand in the mind will become the leading all-suite chain. Move rapidly to dominate the category. To

jump-start the Embassy Suites brand, we suggest you buy the largest chain in the category, Granada Royale, and change its name to Embassy Suites.

Which they did.

2. Hotel suites have the perception of being expensive, and before the launch of all-suite hotels, they were. Embassy Suites, on the other hand, would be reasonable, no more expensive than an ordinary hotel room.

Furthermore, the primary benefit of a suite is to have one room for sleeping and one room for working. Hence our proposed marketing slogan: "Embassy Suites: Two rooms for the price of one."

Which they didn't do.

Our slogan was too simple for management and not at all creative. Instead, they hired another advertising agency that proposed using Garfield, the cartoon cat. Slogan: "You don't have to be a fat cat to enjoy The Suite Life."

Embassy Suites became a very successful brand, thanks primarily to its early lead in the all-suite category. But it missed an opportunity to reposition traditional single-room hotels as too expensive for what you get.

The "two-for-one" slogan could still be effective today. (The all-suite hotels have never achieved the dominance we believe would have been possible in the hotel industry. Many more people stay in traditional single-room hotels than stay in all-suite hotels.)

And Garfield has long since checked out of Embassy Suites.

Marlboro was the first masculine cigarette.
But the key decision that made the brand
the world's best-selling cigarette was
the use of a cowboy as a visual hammer.

CHAPTER 11

Management deals in verbal abstractions. Marketing deals in visual hammers.

Verbally oriented left-brain managers tend to fall in love with abstractions like: "You don't have to be a fat cat to enjoy The Suite Life."

"Fat cat," of course, is a verbal abstraction for an overfed, overpaid corporate executive. And "Suite Life" is a play on the term "sweet life."

The slogan sounds great, but it destroys the visual potential of the Embassy Suites brand. So they settled for the lame visual idea of Garfield.

Visually oriented right-brain marketers want down-to-earth slogans like "Two rooms for the price of one." That idea instantly lends itself to a compelling visual.

What's a UPS?

A senior management person at United Parcel Service asked Al what he thought of the company's new trademark.

"I like it," he said, "but what UPS really needs is a motivating idea or rallying cry, something like 'UPS delivers more parcels to more people in more places than any other company in the world.' "

"UPS," the senior management person said, "is not in the parcel-delivery business."

"Huh. That comes as a big surprise to me. We're a customer, and we always thought that UPS was in the parcel-delivery business."

"No. UPS is in the logistics business."

He wasn't joking. UPS has been repainting some eighty-eight thousand vehicles with its new theme: "Synchronizing the World of Commerce."

(Is UPS thinking of going into the watch business?)

Left-brain managers are verbal, sometimes excessively so. They often elevate their language until their words lose their meanings.

Synchronizing the world of commerce. What does that mean to an average person?

Right-brain marketers are visual. They also deal in words, of course, because the ultimate objective of a marketing program is to own a word in the mind. But they want simple words that can be easily visualized.

What's a financial service?

It would be amusing if the verbal-abstraction problem hadn't become a serious impediment to marketing. Many firms, for example, call themselves "financial services companies."

But how do consumers see the situation?

- If they want to buy banking services, they go to a bank like Bank of America.

- If they want to buy insurance, they go to an insurance company like State Farm.
- If they want to buy stocks, bonds, or mutual funds, they go to a brokerage firm like Merrill Lynch—now a division of Bank of America.

"Let's go to a financial services company to get our finances serviced" is not the way people talk. People talk in terms of specifics, not generalities.

In 1998, Sandy Weill unveiled Citigroup, the biggest financial-services company the world has ever seen. The megamerger combined investment banking, commercial banking, insurance, and fund management.

"A decade later," reported the *New York Times,* "Mr. Weill's watershed deal is regarded by some as one of the worst mergers of all time." A decade later, Citigroup stock was at $24.02, nearly $10 a share lower than the day the deal closed. (Today the stock is at $9.64.)

You might think the Citigroup calamity might have dissuaded other banks from following a similar path. Not so. Next up is Bank of America, which in 2008 bought Countrywide Financial, a troubled subprime mortgage lender, and Merrill Lynch, the nation's largest brokerage firm.

A few more acquisitions like these and Bank of America will be well on its way to becoming the next global financial services company.

You can see the problem. It makes sense to verbally oriented executives to want to build the world's largest financial services company.

But how would you visualize a concept like "financial services"?

The visual hammer.

To build a brand, you need both a nail and a hammer. The verbal is the nail and the visual is the hammer. It's difficult to build a strong brand without both.

Marlboro demonstrates the power of the right combination of a simple verbal and a unique visual. Introduced in the U.S. market in 1953, Marlboro eventually became the world's largest-selling cigarette brand.

Wow! The Marlboro cowboy must be an exceptionally effective visual.

That's not necessarily true. That's not how marketing works. The Marlboro cowboy is only a hammer.

What was the cowboy trying to hammer?

At the time of Marlboro's introduction, virtually all cigarette brands used "unisex" strategies, appealing to both men and women. Virtually all cigarette advertisements featured pictures of women as well as men.

To logical left-brain management types, that made a lot of sense. Cigarette companies figured their future depended on their ability to create as many female smokers as male smokers. (They have almost achieved that goal. Today, 22 percent of adult American women smoke, compared with 28 percent of men.)

Marlboro was conceived as a "masculine" cigarette, one of the first brands to focus entirely on men. (In fifty-five years, there has never been a woman in a Marlboro ad.)

It was this "masculine" verbal that the cowboy hammer was designed to drive into the smoker's mind. It was this combination that built the leadership position for the Marlboro brand.

Interestingly enough, the number one cigarette brand

among American women is also Marlboro. Why is this so? Because many women consider a cigarette to be a "masculine" symbol. By smoking Marlboro, they are asserting masculine characteristics such as aggressiveness and dominance.

Right-brain marketers seldom decide on a verbal without also considering what the visual might be.

Left-brain managers, on the other hand, often settle on such abstract verbal concepts like "quality" or "superior service" or "dependable performance."

But no visual hammer can nail abstract verbal concepts like these into the consumer's mind.

A visual hammer works best with a down-to-earth specific verbal expressed as simply as possible. For example, the first three-blade razor (Mach3) and the first five-blade razor (Fusion) introduced by Gillette.

Yet "nails," or verbal decisions, are often made without consideration of potential "hammers," or visual decisions.

If you can't find a visual device to hammer your verbal nail into the mind, then your strategy tends to fall apart.

A free hammer.

There's one exception to this general rule. When your brand is first in a new category, almost any visual can become an effective visual hammer.

The old-fashioned Coke bottle, for example, is a visual symbol recognized around the world.

When a leader brand like Coca-Cola creates a symbol associated with the category, the number two and number three brands are visually out of luck.

What visual symbol is associated with Pepsi-Cola? None, really.

Mercedes-Benz, the first automobile brand, created the tri-star logotype, which is universally associated with "prestige." Owners don't seem to object when Mercedes uses a one-foot-high logotype in the grille of their automobiles.

Nike, the first athletic shoe, created the Swoosh, not a particularly attractive visual. Yet the Swoosh is a well-known logo around the world in spite of its lack of visual excitement. Why? Because the Swoosh visual is associated with Nike's leadership position.

(Nobody wants to brag about wearing a number two brand.)

McDonald's, the first hamburger chain, created the Golden Arches, another visual hammer with an enormous recognition factor.

Rolex, the first expensive watch, created a visual hammer (a unique watchband) that has since been copied by many competitors. (That didn't hurt Rolex. It just made the other brands looks like "imitation Rolexes.")

Visual hammers are particularly effective for high-end fashion products. They tell friends and relatives how smart (or how dumb) you are. The polo player for the Ralph Lauren brand, for example.

Take ultraexpensive Louis Vuitton handbags. They have a unique multiple-logotype design that anyone can recognize from twenty feet away.

In certain circles, a Louis Vuitton handbag is one of those possessions a woman has to have. In Tokyo, for example, more than 90 percent of women in their twenties own a Louis Vuitton. If the handbag itself weren't quite so "outlandish," sales wouldn't be nearly as high.

Then, too, if Louis Vuitton has captured 90 percent of

young, urban Japanese women, the market share of the number two brand (whatever it is) cannot be too great.

When your brand is first in a new category and you also develop a striking visual hammer to accompany your brand, you can sometimes achieve a near monopoly.

"Nurturing and inspiring the human spirit."

A number of years ago, the management at Starbucks invited a management guru to help it define its "big, hairy, audacious goal."

The company brought together many different people from its management team to participate in the process. They came up with a statement that, according to a former executive, "guides us, anchors us, and inspires us to this day."

The statement: "To be one of the most well-known and respected organizations in the world known for nurturing and inspiring the human spirit."

This might be appropriate for the United States of America, perhaps, but not for a company selling coffee.

To employees, this is just "management talk," which they ignore. When entrepreneur Howard Schultz returned to take the reins of a company that had gone astray, he immediately focused on "coffee."

"Starbucks going back to the bean" was the headline in *USA Today*. "There will be a fundamental change in the taste and experience of going to Starbucks," said Mr. Schultz. "We'll spill out more coffee than most coffee shops sell. You won't be able to find a fresher cup of coffee on the planet."

Left-brain management types talk about "nurturing and inspiring the human spirit." Right-brain entrepreneurs talk about "coffee."

Entrepreneurs such as Howard Schultz, Steve Jobs, Jeff Bezos, Michael Dell, and Dietrich Mateschitz, in our opinion, are fundamentally right-brain marketing types.

When entrepreneurs grow up, however, they often fall into a management mode and let their left-brain subordinates take over.

"We've been robbed. Call the law-enforcement officers."

That's not a likely scenario. The average person is much more likely to say, "We've been robbed. Call the cops."

Unfortunately, left-brain management people are not average people. They often complicate the work of their marketing people by their constant upgrading of language. Not only does a term have to be politically correct, it also has to be as long and as complicated as possible.

- Maintenance men are now physical plant managers.
- Janitors are now custodial engineers.
- A business strategy is now a business model.
- Accounting firms are now professional service firms.
- The purchasing department is now the procurement department.
- The personnel department is now the human relations department.

At Electronic Data Systems, the human relations department moved one step up the abstraction ladder and became the "Leadership and Change Management" department.

The specific vs. the general.

People know that a drugstore sells more than just drugs. It also sells toiletries, cosmetics, school supplies, greeting cards, magazines, candy, soft drinks, snacks, stationery, and photo supplies, among other items.

Should a drugstore call itself a "personal-items" store? We think not.

In every aspect of life, the consumer prefers the narrow, specific word to the broader, more general word.

Furthermore, consumers assume that a specific word has a more general meaning.

- A gas station sells more than just gas.
- A coffee shop sells more than just coffee.
- A steak house sells more than just steak.
- Taco Bell sells more than just tacos.
- Burger King sells more than just burgers.
- Red Lobster sells more than just lobster.

Should Burger King call itself "Fast-Food King"? Should Red Lobster call itself "Red Seafood"?

In every case, the specific is more poetic and more memorable than the general.

The visual advantage of the specific.

Consumers know that a suitcase is designed to hold more than just "suits." So why isn't a suitcase called a "clothing case"?

The more specific the word, the easier it is to associate the word with a visual. You can easily visualize a "suit," but to visualize "clothing" is a lot more difficult.

A simple word combined with a visual sticks in the mind much better than a complicated word without a visual.

Burger King and Red Lobster are good names because a "burger" is easier to visualize than "fast food." A "lobster" is easier to visualize than "seafood."

One reason "The ultimate driving machine" is a great slogan is that it's relatively easy to visualize the thrill of driving a BMW on a winding road.

One reason "Moving forward" is a lousy slogan for Toyota is that there's no way to visualize the idea. It's typical management talk. "We are not standing still. We are always moving forward to achieve automotive excellence."

A third of General Electric's business is in what it calls its "infrastructure" segment. Does the average person have any idea what "infrastructure" is? Is there any way to visualize a complicated idea like infrastructure?

The History Channel has just changed its name to History. How is an employee going to answer a common question like "Where do you work?"

"At History?"

What's a Market?

When it first opened its doors, Boston Chicken was a huge hit. It was the first fast-food restaurant chain to focus on rotisserie chicken for the take-home dinner market.

But then it added turkey, meat loaf, ham, and other items to the menu and changed its name to Boston Market.

Everybody knows what a chicken dinner is, but what's a "market" dinner? No wonder the company went bankrupt. "Rotisserie chicken" is easy to visualize. "Market" is not.

Everyone knows advertising agencies do a lot more than just advertising. So why aren't they called "marketing agencies"?

Again, it's easy to visual an "advertisement." But how do you visualize "marketing"?

You probably know many famous advertising agencies, but how many famous marketing-communications agencies do you know? Name one.

Right-brain marketing people know they need to use the narrowest possible term to describe a brand or a category so they can develop an effective visual hammer.

Now, if there were only a way to get that message to management.

Capturing more than 50 percent of a market
almost always requires multiple brands.
Gillette's seven brands account for 71 percent
of the global wet-shaving market.

CHAPTER 12

Management prefers a single brand.
Marketing prefers multiple brands.

On the surface, management wins this round hands down. In an overcommunicated society, why not put all your sales and marketing resources behind a single brand?

And some successful companies that do just that. General Electric, IBM, Microsoft, and others.

Every one of these companies, however, lost a bundle when they tried to use the house name on a new product or service outside its core business.

- General Electric and mainframe computers
- IBM and personal computers
- Microsoft and Internet search

On the other hand, there are many hugely successful companies that have multiple brands—Procter & Gamble being a typical example.

The world's most magnificent marketing machine.

In the last few decades, Procter & Gamble has launched many successful brands. These include Vicks, Oil of Olay, Pantene, Cover Girl, Noxzema, Clarion, Old Spice, Max Factor, Giorgio, Baby Fresh, Tampax, Iams, Spinbrush, Clairol, Wella, and Glide.

Wait a minute, you might be thinking. Didn't P&G buy Glide from W.L. Gore and Wella from a German company?

That's right. It did. As a matter of fact, Procter & Gamble bought all sixteen of those brands and relaunched them as P&G brands.

That's what most big companies do. Instead of launching their own brands, they buy them from other companies, sometimes for a lot of money. The Wella deal cost P&G a reported 6.5 billion euros.

And in 2005, Procter & Gamble bought Gillette for $57 billion in stock, scooping up the Gillette, Duracell, Braun, and Oral-B brands.

We have a lot of respect for the marketing savvy of the people at P&G. In books and articles, we have commented favorably on the strategies developed for many of their brands—the launches of Crest toothpaste and Scope mouthwash in particular.

Why doesn't P&G launch its own brands?

With all of Procter & Gamble's financial muscle and marketing smarts, why does it need to buy brands?

Having worked with many large companies, we know it is difficult to get management to launch a new brand.

Invariably, management wants to "wait and see" if a market develops. Or it wants to launch line-extensions of one of the company's existing brands.

The last major brand launched by Procter & Gamble was Whitestrips in 2001. Even then, the company didn't have the courage to give the new product a totally new name. Rather, it hung the Crest name on Whitestrips, even though the product has nothing to do with toothpaste.

Why? Research suggested that consumers would have more confidence in Whitestrips if it also had the Crest name on the package than if it had a totally new name.

Left-brain management believes in research while many right-brain marketing people do not. When you research a known name (Crest) against an unknown name, the known name is almost always going to win. (Suppose Google had researched the Google name before launching its Web site.)

Big companies don't launch "Google-type" names because they don't test well. But you might be thinking, "Don't marketing people initiate these name-research projects?"

Sure, they do. But, in general, they do so only because they know management won't approve the launch of a new brand without research. And the new name never tests well, so the company goes with a line extension.

The biggest killer of new brands.

Recently, Procter & Gamble introduced a new line of high-end coffees. The new name: Folgers Gourmet Selections.

Years ago, suppose they had tested the Folgers Gourmet name against a unique brand name like Starbucks? Folgers would have been the big winner in our opinion.

Before Dietrich Mateschitz introduced Red Bull, he tested the name and the concept. "People didn't believe the taste, the logo, the brand name. I've never before experienced such a disaster."

But Mr. Mateschitz introduced Red Bull anyway, something that a right-brain entrepreneur would do, but not something that most big companies would do.

Rarely do big companies use unique, distinctive, unusual brand names such as Yahoo!, Amazon, Yellow Tail, Crocs, Grey Goose, Apple, and BlackBerry. Unique, distinctive, unusual brand names don't test well.

This is not an indictment of the left brainers at P&G. Most big companies do the same. As a result, they wind up buying brands rather than launching them.

PepsiCo bought Mountain Dew and Gatorade, for example, instead of launching its own caffeinated citrus and sports drinks.

(Actually, PepsiCo did launch a sports drink, All Sport, which went nowhere. The problem was that the company waited twenty-seven years before getting into the market. Gatorade was launched in 1967, and All Sport and Coca-Cola's Powerade weren't launched until 1994.)

You can't give the competition a twenty-seven-year head start and expect to build a dominant brand. So PepsiCo spent $13 billion to buy the real thing: Gatorade, along with its corporate parent, Quaker Oats.

The Procter & Gamble of soft drinks.

That's Coca-Cola. But the company is no better at launching new brands than P&G.

Coca-Cola missed the caffeinated citrus category (pioneered by Mountain Dew), so it tried to get into the game with Mello Yello. That didn't work. So it tried Surge, which didn't work, either.

Coca-Cola missed the spicy cola category (pioneered by

Dr Pepper), so it tried to get into the game with Mr. Pibb. That didn't work, either.

Coca-Cola missed the all-natural category (pioneered by Snapple), so it tried to get into the game with Fruitopia. That didn't work, either.

And, of course, Coca-Cola missed the sports-drink category (pioneered by Gatorade) and the energy-drink category (pioneered by Red Bull).

The last leader brand introduced by the Coca-Cola Company was Sprite, introduced in 1961. But it wasn't until 1989 that Sprite passed 7UP to become the number one selling carbonated lemon-and-lime drink.

One reason for Sprite's marketing victory: Coke leaned on its bottlers to drop 7UP and replace it with Sprite.

When to launch a new brand.

Whenever a fashion or technological change occurs, an existing brand, no matter how dominant, faces a choice.

Should the existing brand be "stretched" to encompass the new fashion or the new technology? Or should the company launch a new brand?

If the change is significant enough, the better answer is almost always "launch a new brand."

- The rise of casual clothing in the workplace led Levi Strauss to introduce Dockers, which has become a billion-dollar worldwide brand.
- The success of Mercedes-Benz and BMW led Toyota to introduce Lexus, which has become the largest-selling luxury vehicle in the United States.
- The success of Makita, a Japanese professional-tool

brand, led Black & Decker to introduce DeWalt, which has become the dominant U.S. brand in the professional-tool category.

- The success of Costco led Wal-Mart to introduce Sam's Club, which is now neck and neck with the category leader.

When it comes to launching successful second brands, you rapidly run out of case histories. By far the majority of companies prefer to expand their core brand to cover an emerging new category—usually with mediocre success.

Some examples:

- IBM's failure to extend its mainframe dominance to the personal-computer field.
- Xerox's failure to extend its copier dominance to the computer field.
- Polaroid's failure to move its brand out of instant photography.
- Kodak's failure to duplicate its film-photography success in the digital field.

Every one of these cases, in our opinion, called for a new brand name. Yet all four of these companies tried to extend their existing brands into new categories. Paradoxically, the stronger the brand name, the harder this is to do.

Why is a strong brand name more difficult to move than a weak one? It has to do with the human mind. Strong brand names are deeply embedded in the mind. Weak brands are not.

(But there's usually no point in extending a weak brand.)

Paying a high price for a line extension.

Companies that shy away from second brands often end up paying a high price. The latest victims of second-brand skittishness are Visa Inc. and MasterCard Incorporated. So far, it has cost the two credit-card companies $3 billion, with possibly more financial bad news to come.

A number of years ago, the two credit-card giants decided to get into the debit-card business. It would be hard to find two categories that are more competitive. Credit cards are the enemy of debit cards. And vice versa.

So what did Visa and MasterCard do? They put the same names on both cards—Visa on credit cards and Visa on debit cards. And MasterCard did the same.

To compound the problem, both companies forced their retailers to "honor all cards." In other words, if a retailer accepts a Visa credit card, the retailer must also accept a Visa debit card.

Then they put the debit-card charges through the same signature-based system as the credit-card charges, forcing the retailer to pay five to ten times as much in fees as it would if the customer used one of the alternate debit-card networks, such as Star, Pulse, or NYCE, which use a system based on a personal identification number, or PIN.

In the biggest antitrust settlement in history, Visa agreed to pay $2 billion and MasterCard $1 billion to a group of retailers led by Wal-Mart. Their contention: "Honor all cards" was an illegal tie-in scheme.

Why didn't the credit-card giants launch debit-card brands?

It's the chicken-and-egg problem, explained one Visa

executive. Visa would have had to start a new brand from scratch, one not yet issued by any bank or honored by any merchant. "But why would you possibly have done that?"

That's logical thinking, of course. But a marketer intuitively knows that a second category needs a second brand.

MasterCard's second-brand strategy.

Actually, MasterCard did launch a PIN product called Maestro (not exactly a world-class name.) But Maestro was losing out to the Visa signature debit card, so MasterCard reversed course and launched a line extension.

Too bad. If MasterCard had had a little more faith in its strategy, today it would have been a billion dollars richer and would have had a big lead over its Visa competition in PIN-based debit cards.

Like many marketing problems, the debit-card situation is complicated. How do you design a product that has benefits for all the players in the game? Consumers, retailers, banks, and the card network itself? It's not easy.

Here is where the power of right-brain conceptual thinking comes in. Categories tend to diverge, not converge. You may not know how, when, or where that divergence will take place, but you can be sure that ultimately it will.

Two categories, credit cards and debit cards, will become more and more different, and there's nothing one company can do about it. Trying to keep them together under the same brand name is an exercise in futility.

Never fight a trend. As time goes on, there's always going to be room for new brands. If you don't launch a second brand, you can be sure that one of your competitors will.

Why do the left-brain thinkers at big companies miss the boat when it comes to launching new brands? There are three reasons.

1. An advertising-driven launch.

Big-company management will generally not launch a new brand without backing it with a substantial advertising budget. Yet a successful new brand is usually built around a new category, which can take years to develop.

That's why many successful new brands started slowly, using primarily PR techniques: Starbucks, Google, eBay, Airborne, and Zagat's, to name a few.

These brands and many others were introduced by entrepreneurs who had the patience to hang in there until their markets developed.

Any big company that took a look at Red Bull in its early days would have said, "There's no market there. We can't afford the big advertising budget necessary to launch an energy-drink brand."

By the time the market develops, it's too late for a me-too brand.

2. A research-driven name.

You can't create a new category with a line-extension name. Invariably, new categories are dominated by new names created especially for the category. Red Bull, not Ari-Zona Extreme Energy. PowerBar, not Gatorade Energy Bar. Amazon.com, not BarnesandNoble.com. Xerox, not IBM copiers. Dell, not IBM personal computers.

With marketing history clearly in favor of new names

rather than "stretched" names, why do companies continue to take the line-extension path?

Research.

When asked which brand name he or she prefers, the average consumer invariably chooses the familiar name.

Toyota Super or Lexus? Invariably, the answer would have been Toyota Super. Who ever heard of a Lexus?

(Either Toyota neglected to research the Lexus name or it chose to ignore its own research.)

3. A broad distribution plan.

With a substantial advertising launch, a new product needs broad distribution to make the economics work. So companies pressure the distribution with discounts, two-for-ones, free merchandise, and often the payment of slotting fees.

The odds are stacked against such a plan. New brands take off slowly, and with little selling at point of sale, most new product launches are bound to fail.

(A recent Nielsen BASES and Ernst & Young study put the failure rate of new U.S. consumer products at 95 percent and new European consumer products at 90 percent.)

A better distribution plan is to start "narrow," often with a single chain. Charles Shaw (Two-Buck Chuck) started with a single chain (Trader Joe's) in a single state (California) and became the fastest-growing table wine ever.

Newman's Own salad dressing was launched in a single supermarket (Stew Leonard's in Norwalk, Connecticut). The store sold ten thousand bottles in the first two weeks.

With narrow distribution, you can often arrange special displays and promotions, which increase your brand's chance for long-term success.

Multiple brands are not for everybody.

In our consulting work, we find that most large companies strongly resist the idea of launching new brands.

On the other hand, most small companies seem eager to launch second and third brands. They seem to feel that they are more likely to succeed if they have more than one horse in the race.

Not true. A small company needs to concentrate all of its resources (especially management's time) on a single product or service, even if it has to throw away a good idea from time to time.

A small company is especially vulnerable to competition. The way to fend off competitors is to make your brand bigger and stronger so that you dominate your category.

Then you can launch a second brand.

Old packaging.

New packaging.

ITALY'S #1 BRAND OF PASTA

Barilla boxes used to feature its credentials
with a big "#1" in a gold seal one-inch high.
Today, the brand's credentials are buried in
a line of type one-sixteenth of an inch high.

CHAPTER 13

Management values cleverness.
Marketing values credentials.

In their *BusinessWeek* column, Jack Welch and his wife, Suzy, responded to the question "What are some of the best approaches to improving marketing?"

They cited "two great campaigns that ran in connection with the World Series. In the first, a Boston retailer, Jordan's, promised to give away all the furniture it sold last April if the Red Sox won in October." (They did.)

"In the second, Taco Bell promised to give a taco to everyone in America if a base was stolen in the series." (It was.)

"When all is said and done," noted the Welches, "a clever idea can still score big."

Free furniture and free tacos might impress management types, but not marketing. Marketing is not about cleverness. Marketing is about consistency and credentials.

A slick marketer?

What confuses the situation is the media's tendency to refer to failed CEOs as "marketing types."

Here's how Carly Fiorina was described after she was fired from Hewlett-Packard.

- "A slick marketer"—*USA Today*
- "A high-powered marketing whiz"—*Newsweek*
- "A sales whiz known for high-profile marketing events"—*BusinessWeek*
- "Carly tried to impose . . . a marketing culture on a company with an entrenched engineering culture"
  —*New York Times*

As far as we can determine, Ms. Fiorina had little or no marketing experience before getting the top HP job. Apparently, her flamboyance convinced editors she was marketing material.

One example of her antimarketing instincts is her introduction of 158 new HP products at a single, heavily promoted press conference in 2003.

Would Steve Jobs have introduced the iPod and the iPhone and 156 other new Apple products at a single press event? One at a time is good right-brain-marketing thinking. An individual brand can get famous, but a crowd can't get.

"Synergies," said Ms. Fiorina, "would eventually make HP a leader in all of its businesses." What marketing expert runs around the country talking about synergies? Only left-brain CEOs and investment bankers do that.

A slick marketer? Our tastes run more toward Sidney Frank, who, at age seventy-seven, launched Grey Goose vodka.

Or John Schnatter, who in his early twenties started selling pizza, tearing out a broom closet to put a pie oven in a bar co-owned by his father in Jeffersonville, Indiana. Ten years later, the company went public as Papa John's Pizza.

Or Gary Heavin, who sold his first Curves franchise in 1995 and now has a franchised chain with eight thousand locations and more than $1 billion in annual revenues.

With her enthusiasm, energy, and drive, Carly Fiorina might have made a fine CEO of Hewlett-Packard . . . if she had a marketing expert behind her whispering in her ear.

There's nothing slick about marketing. If it sounds "slick," it's probably the wrong thing to do.

"Soul of the Earth."

In a previous book, *The Fall of Advertising & the Rise of PR,* we discussed the positioning of the country of Guatemala. Since then, Guatemala has launched a new tourist strategy. The theme: Soul of the Earth.

If you were the president of Guatemala, would you think this was a good idea or not?

How does a management person decide whether a marketing idea is good or not?

Too many logical left brainers make decisions based on how ideas affect them personally. "I like it." Or "I don't like it." What usually tips the scales is the "surprise" factor: "Never thought of that."

Changing one vowel from *i* to *u* converts "soil of the earth" into "Soul of the Earth," a totally new idea. "What a clever play on words."

Marketing people look for credentials, not cleverness.

What should Guatemala's new tourist strategy be? Actually, the country has a rich heritage. It was the cultural center of the Maya, the most advanced civilization in all of North and South America before the arrival of the Spanish.

Even today, 43 percent of Guatemala's population of 13 million people are of Mayan descent. Many still speak dialects of the Mayan language.

With mountain ranges as high as ten thousand feet and a culture seemingly unchanged for five hundred years, Guatemala is a tourist paradise. Scattered throughout Guatemala are hundreds of spectacular Mayan ruins. Cities, temples, houses, playing fields.

The relics of a glorious past. More historic than the Pyramids of Egypt or the Taj Mahal of India, and built for the living rather than the dead.

There's one problem, however. Even though Guatemala was the center of Mayan civilization, there are Mayan ruins scattered over Belize, El Salvador, western Honduras, and southern Mexico. (Even worse, in Mexico's Yucatán Peninsula, a tourism district has been formed to promote "Riviera Maya.")

Besides the Maya confusion, there's also the country confusion. In addition to Guatemala, Belize, El Salvador, and Honduras, there are three other countries in Central America: Costa Rica, Nicaragua, and Panama. It's going to be hard for the average consumer to associate "Maya" with just one of these seven countries.

How do you solve the country confusion problem? You change the name of the country from Guatemala to Guatemaya.

The visual hammer: a Mayan temple.

The single word "Guatemaya" preempts the Mayan position and serves as a memory device to link the Maya to the country in Central America where the most spectacular Mayan ruins can be found.

Changing the name also makes sense from another point of view. When Spanish conquistador Pedro de Alvarado asked his Aztec guide, "What do you call this land?" the guide replied *"Quauhtemallan,"* meaning "land of trees."

Guatemala is actually a word derived from the Aztec language rather than the language of the native population of the country.

"Soul of the Earth" or "Center of Maya Civilization"? The two approaches to developing a marketing strategy. Cleverness versus credentials. Left brainers versus right brainers.

People don't think in a vacuum.

They accept or reject a new idea not just on its merits but also on whether the new idea fits in with all the other ideas they have accumulated over the years.

A new cola brand, for example, has to fit in with everything the cola drinker thinks about Coca-Cola and Pepsi-Cola.

One way to determine whether a new idea will make its way into consumers' minds is to reverse the idea and see if it applies to the competition.

Take the Avis program, selected by *Advertising Age* as the tenth-best advertising campaign of the twentieth century. "Avis is No.2 in rent-a-cars, so why go with us? We try harder."

Reverse the idea and you have "Hertz is No.1 in rent-a-cars, so they don't have to try as hard." Sounds reasonable to prospects, so they buy into the Avis position.

Take the De Beers slogan "A diamond is forever" and reverse it. "Other gemstones won't last as long because they're not as hard as a diamond." Sounds right to most people.

Most marketing strategies fail miserably on the reversal test.

Take American Airlines' slogan "We know why you fly" and reverse it. "Other airlines don't know why you fly"?

Come on, American. Every airline knows why we fly, but what you need to figure out is why we should fly American. Or Delta. Or United.

Take Delta Air Lines' "Good goes around" and reverse it. At other airlines, "Bad goes around"?

Clever, but not credible.

Italy's #1 pasta.

In 1996, three years after Barilla was introduced into the U.S. market, the brand became the No. 1 pasta in America.

Not bad, considering the competition: Ronzoni, Mueller's, Creamette, San Giorgia, and American Beauty, among others. The previous market leader (Ronzoni) was owned by Hershey Foods, a formidable marketing company.

Today, Barilla has 26 percent of the U.S. pasta market, more than twice the share of the No. 2 brand, even though Barilla often sells for 5 to 10 percent more.

The idea that drove Barilla to the top: "Italy's #1 pasta." How clever is that?

Furthermore, Barilla is produced in Ames, Iowa, with a second plant recently opened in Avon, New York. That's a long way from Barilla headquarters in Parma, the capital of Italy's "food valley." (That's why the Barilla slogan was recently changed to "Italy's #1 *brand* of pasta.")

Traditional wisdom would credit Barilla's success to

the barrage of thirty-second television commercials that launched the brand. An American woman makes eye contact with a mysterious Italian stranger who serves her Barilla pasta, all set to vocals by tenor Andrea Bocelli.

Many commercials take a similar approach. They focus on creating a rapport with consumers in order to build loyalty to the brand. There's a certain "warm-and-fuzzy" feeling in a typical TV spot. The objective is to make the consumer fall in love with the brand.

The soft sell is in; the hard sell is out.

The missing ingredient.

There's nothing wrong with this approach, provided you add one additional ingredient: credentials.

For example, "Italy's #1 pasta."

Subtract the credentials from the commercials and you have nothing but mush. Beautiful, enchanting, romantic mush.

Much advertising is mush, especially television advertising. Thirty expensive seconds wasted trying to proposition the viewer without providing the credentials for the consumer to take the offer seriously.

Management often confuses cause and effect. Sure, every company wants the consumer to fall in love with its brands. Sure, every company wants to build brand preference, loyalty, and all those other mushy attributes. That's the effect the company wants to create. But what's the cause?

Invariably, the cause is some variation of the brand's credentials. "It must be good because it's Italy's No. 1 pasta." Not: "It must be good because the company ran a wonderful commercial."

A good television commercial is like a good pasta dish,

which is mostly mush (the pasta) with the taste concentrated in the sauce.

A good TV commercial is also mostly mush (the story line) with the motivation concentrated in the brand's credentials.

What every brand needs.

Behind almost every successful brand is some aspect of the brand's credentials.

- The brand was first in a new category (Viagra and erectile dysfunction).
- The brand was first with a new technology (Velcro and hook-and-loop construction).
- The brand was first in a segment of a day (NyQuil, the nighttime cold remedy).
- The brand was first in a segment of a category (Prius and hybrid vehicles).
- The brand was first to claim a new attribute (Geox, the shoe that breathes).
- The brand was first to be endorsed by an influential third party (Movado, the museum watch, in the permanent collection of the Museum of Modern Art).
- The brand was the first to be imported from a country identified with the category (Stolichnaya, the Russian vodka).

After a brand becomes established, however, a company often drops the brand's credentials. Big mistake. Credentials are what built the brand. Credentials should always play a major role in the marketing of a brand.

What built the Federal Express brand? Overnight delivery. "FedEx this package to L.A." means "Get this package to Los Angeles by tomorrow morning."

Like many other companies, the management at FedEx has dropped its credentials. No mention of overnight service, just a long line of "credential-less" themes like "The world on time" and "Relax . . . it's FedEx."

Keep tuned. "Italy's #1 pasta" is likely to go the way of "When it absolutely, positively has to be there overnight."

What should FedEx advertising say?

"When it absolutely, positively has to be there overnight." Those are the company's credentials.

Sure, today FedEx has other services, including two and three-day deliveries. But if it does a terrific job on overnight delivery, it must be pretty good at those other services, too.

Management vs. marketing principles.

James Wetherbe wrote a book, *The World on Time*, outlining the eleven management principles that made FedEx a big success.

Do you suppose any one of those principles had anything to do with narrowing the focus to overnight service?

Of course not. Those are "management" principles, not marketing principles.

Joseph Michelli wrote a book, *The Starbucks Experience,* outlining the "5 Principles for Turning Ordinary into Extraordinary."

1. Make it your own.
2. Everything matters.
3. Surprise and delight.
4. Embrace resistance.
5. Leave your mark.

Whatever happened to being first in something? But, again, these are management principles, not marketing principles.

Howard Behar, a former president of Starbucks International, wrote a book, *It's Not About the Coffee,* explaining his "Leadership Principles from a Life at Starbucks."

By now, you get the picture. Management principles are almost never about strategy, but almost always about execution.

"In real life, strategy is actually very straightforward," wrote Jack Welch. "You pick a general direction and implement like hell."

Or as Lou Gerstner said, "Strategy is execution." Or as Larry Bossidy and Ram Charan wrote in their best-selling book, *Execution*: "So much thinking has gone into strategy that it's no longer an intellectual challenge. You can rent any strategy you want from a consulting firm."

Execution is "the biggest issue facing business today."

Who's at fault for mushy marketing?

Left-brain management or right-brain marketing? It's easy to blame advertising agencies, PR agencies, advertising managers, and marketing managers for the mushiness you find in almost all marketing messages.

It's been our experience, however, that the marketing buck stops on the CEO's desk. The company's chief executive might not approve the individual advertisements or commercials, but he or she generally approves the direction and slogan of the marketing campaign.

There's the rub. Years ago, famed researcher Alfred Politz pointed out the pitfalls that occur when clients demand clever advertising. "It is unfortunate, but not surprising, that the creative man now diverts his efforts from making the product interesting to making the advertising interesting."

"Ultimately he is no longer selling the product to the consumer," stated Politz, "but selling the advertising to his client."

What's interesting to the client may not be relevant to the prospect. Put yourself in the boardroom of a typical big company in America. "We'd like to go back," says the agency presenter, "and rerun an advertising campaign that built the brand decades ago."

It never happens. "We're spending millions of dollars and you want to recycle an old advertising slogan? We could do that ourselves. What are we paying you for?"

Nothing is as dead as yesterday's advertising slogan.

"The real thing."

This is the one idea indelibly embedded in the minds of cola drinkers since it was first used by Coca-Cola in 1969.

These are Coca-Cola's credentials. In three words, the phrase communicates the fact that Coca-Cola is the first cola, the authentic cola, and everything else is an imitation of the real thing.

This is the motivating reason to prefer Coca-Cola. How can Pepsi-Cola or Royal Crown be better than the real thing?

Many brands could have used the same concept, but didn't. Kleenex is the real thing in tissue. Heinz is the real thing in ketchup. Hellmann's is the real thing in mayonnaise.

Coca-Cola has preempted the concept, yet refuses to use it. Strange indeed. Instead, Coca-Cola careens from one marketing campaign to the next, none of which are related to each other and none of which touch base with the brand's credentials.

The Coca-Cola Company spent millions on an ad campaign called "Always." Yet go into a bar and ask for an "Always" and you'll see a bewildered look on the face of the bartender. But ask for "The real thing" and you'll get a Coke.

When you own "The real thing," why would you run advertising programs with themes like these.

- "Polar bears."
- "Always."
- "Enjoy."
- "Life tastes good."
- "All the world loves a Coke."
- "The Coke side of life."

"You can't argue with success," you might be thinking. "Coca-Cola is the world's most valuable brand."

But is Coca-Cola the dominant brand it appears to be?

In the U.S. market, here's how some leading brands compare with the number two brands in their categories.

- Marlboro leads Newport by 397 percent.
- Budweiser leads Miller by 156 percent.
- McDonald's leads Burger King by 133 percent.
- Visa leads MasterCard by 96 percent.
- But Coca-Cola, the world's most valuable brand, leads Pepsi-Cola by only 61 percent.

"Hotlanta."

In 2005, Mayor Shirley Franklin announced the launch of a public and private initiative "to create a new, compelling branding strategy and marketing campaign for Atlanta."

After eight months of gestation, the new logotype and slogan for the Brand Atlanta campaign was introduced: "Every day is an opening day."

Every day is an opening day? What is this, show business? Sounds like Broadway or Las Vegas to us.

What leads cities, states, countries, and companies to concoct meaningless, unmemorable slogans? We believe the culprit is "cleverness" or "creativity."

Look at the guidelines issued to the Brand Atlanta task force. The objective was "to create a new, compelling branding strategy."

Every day of the week, advertising agencies are hired to create new, compelling branding strategies and fired when these new, compelling branding strategies don't work.

Why in the world would anyone want a new strategy when it already has an existing strategy? The day we moved to Atlanta from New York, Doug Billian, an old friend of ours, called and said, "Welcome to Hotlanta."

Hotlanta is widely associated with the city, especially since the 1996 Summer Olympics. Furthermore, the city itself is booming.

- From 2000 to 2006, Metro Atlanta added 890,000 residents, the largest numerical gain of the nation's 361 metropolitan areas.
- In 2005, Atlanta registered 72,861 new private-housing

starts, the largest in the nation. (New York City was second. Phoenix was third.)

- Atlanta leads the country in luring highly educated twenty-five- to thirty-four-year-olds, a group demographers call the "Young and Restless."
- Atlanta's Hartsfield-Jackson airport is the world's busiest, handling the most takeoffs and landings and the most passengers.

So well known is the Hotlanta idea that Coca-Cola ran a local billboard campaign with a frosty bottle of Coke and the words: "Welcome to Coldlanta."

"Every day is an opening day." What folly. After two years and a multimillion-dollar expenditure, the campaign was quietly killed.

New slogan: "City lights. Southern nights." Just as bad.

Like every product or service or city or state, it's a credentials issue. Atlanta has the credentials to market itself as "Hotlanta." Other cities don't.

But every city has opening days, lights, and nights. No matter how clever these ideas may be, they won't work. They are ideas built on sand, not on a sound foundation.

"A diamond is forever."

One of the longest-running (and most effective) marketing campaigns is the one first used by De Beers in 1948.

Notice the double entendre, always a good idea in a slogan. If a diamond lasts forever, so will a marriage solemnized with a diamond engagement ring and a diamond wedding ring.

So what did De Beers do recently? You guessed it. They changed the slogan to "Forever, now."

Not only is "Forever, now" a non sequitur but it also has no meaning unless you connect it with the original slogan.

The three most important rules of advertising used to be (1) repetition, (2) repetition, and (3) repetition.

Today, management seems to have forgotten these rules. Today, it seems like the three most important rules are (1) cleverness, (2) novelty, and (3) gimmickry.

Some of the most successful marketing programs have been the ones that have run for decades, not years.

It took twenty-five years of cowboy consistency before Marlboro passed Winston to become the number one selling cigarette in the United States.

Marlboro was the brand that made Philip Morris a hugely successful company. If you had invested $1,000 in Philip Morris stock at the end of 1953, the year Marlboro was introduced, your stake would be worth $15 million today.

(As a matter of fact, Philip Morris stock appreciated faster than any other stock on *Fortune* magazine's list that year of the five hundred largest U.S. industrial companies.)

Suppose that early in the game some new CEO arrived at Philip Morris and said, "I'm tired of cowboys. Why can't we use football players?"

That's not as far-fetched as you might think. "Every five or seven years," says PepsiCo's CEO Indra Nooyi, "you've got to change out the approach to the brand, because you need a new boost of energy to think about the next iteration." (That kind of thinking helped to kill the highly successful "Pepsi Generation" campaign.)

Few companies stay the course.

Has Mercedes-Benz made any real progress in enhancing its brand since it dropped its longtime slogan "Engineered like no other car in the world?" We think not.

Has the U.S. Army made any recruiting progress since it dropped its longtime slogan "Be all you can be" and substituted "An army of one"? We think not. (New slogan: "Army strong.")

Has Budweiser enhanced its brand since it dropped "King of beers"? We think not.

New York City is the "Big Apple." Paris is the "City of Light." Rome is the "Eternal City." Nashville is the "Music City." Minnesota is the "Land of 10,000 Lakes." Would you change any of these marketing slogans? We think not.

A number of years ago, the *Minneapolis Tribune* sponsored a contest to develop a new slogan to replace "Land of 10,000 Lakes." The winner: "Come fall in love with a loon." (Cleverness at its looniest.)

It was N. W. Ayer, an agency that can trace its history to the first advertising agency founded in America, that coined the motto "Keeping everlastingly at it brings success."

It was also N. W. Ayer that coined the slogan "A diamond is forever."

Every year, the number of brands that keep everlastingly at it, as far as marketing slogans are concerned, continues to decline, a situation you can blame on the cleverness crowd.

A slogan is forever.

After it became the leading freeze-dried coffee,
Taster's Choice was saddled with the
"Nescafé" name. That makes no sense.
Two names are not better than one.

CHAPTER 14

Management believes in double branding.
Marketing believes in single branding.

Branding is getting so popular in the boardroom today that left-brain management tends to overdo it.

"If one brand is good," goes the thinking, "then two must be better." (A logical conclusion that makes sense, but it can undermine a brand.)

Many chief executives are busy putting their corporate names on all of their brands. Are CEOs doing this to boost their stocks or are they doing it to boost their brands? One wonders.

Double branding is resisted by many right-brain marketing people for one reason. When given a choice, consumers will invariably use one name instead of two.

Nescafé Taster's Choice.

Years ago, Taster's Choice overtook Maxim to become the number one freeze-dried coffee in America. One reason was its superior name. Taster's Choice implied a benefit.

The brand name Maxim implied that the coffee was a

product of Maxwell House, the country's leading coffee brand at the time. (Another line-extension mistake.)

The seldom-told story of the Taster's Choice name is the fact that the Nestlé management in Switzerland wanted to call the product Nescafé Gold to take advantage of Nescafé, the world's largest-selling instant coffee. (In essence, making the same mistake as Maxim.)

U.S. marketing people, on the other hand, insisted on the Taster's Choice name and eventually won the internal as well as the external battle.

Well, the folks in Vevey finally got their way. Since 2003, Taster's Choice is officially Nescafé Taster's Choice.

But what do consumers call the product? They don't call it by its full name, Nescafé Taster's Choice. That's just too long and cumbersome. They don't call it Nescafé. That's the name of another coffee brand.

Consumers call the product Taster's Choice. The same name they have always used. The double branding just adds a confusing element to the package.

Kleenex Cottonelle.

In spite of the dubious advantages of double branding, there's no question it's a trend. At Procter & Gamble, Glide became Crest Glide. SpinBrush became Crest SpinBrush. A new mouthwash became Crest Pro-Health.

At Kimberly-Clark, Cottonelle is now Kleenex Cottonelle.

With the acquisition of Gillette, Procter & Gamble is starting to integrate the two companies' brands. A new toothbrush is called the Oral-B CrossAction ProHealth, a name that's a mouthful.

Consumers, however, will usually use one name instead of

two. Nobody in their right mind would write Nescafé Taster's Choice on a shopping list. Or Crest Glide. Or Kleenex Cottonelle. It's just Taster's Choice, Glide, and Cottonelle.

But what single name could consumers use for Oral-B CrossAction ProHealth toothbrush? The Oral-B name is used on sixteen different toothbrush products. The CrossAction name is used on three different toothbrush products. And Pro-Health is both a toothpaste and a mouthwash.

No wonder consumers wandering around drugstores today look confused.

The strongest brands are those that stand on their own, without corporate endorsements or master branding. If Nestlé bought Red Bull (an acquisition they should definitely consider), should the brand be rebadged as Nestlé Red Bull? We think not.

Single words make strong brands.

Strong brands like Absolut, Amazon, Barbie, BlackBerry, Dell, Duracell, Gatorade, Google, Kleenex, Listerine, Microsoft, Rolex, Sprite, Subway, Tylenol, Xerox, and Zara.

Adding a corporate endorsement to these (and many other single-word or single-concept brands) would weaken them, not strengthen them.

Procter & Gamble's Duracell is not going to attract any additional buyers to its Duracell battery brand.

What about Apple? Look at what Apple's corporate endorsement has done for its iPod brand, you might be thinking.

It's the opposite. Look at what the success of the iPod brand has done for the reputation of Apple. The iPod is the brand name of Apple's music player. Apple is nothing more than a corporate endorsement that the iPod didn't need when it was introduced and doesn't need now.

We have never met a single person who refers to his or her music player as an Apple. Nobody says, "I just bought an Apple," unless they have just bought an apple. On the other hand, plenty of people do say, "I just bought an iPod."

The same is true of many other double-branded products. Nobody calls his or her video-game consoles Sony. They call them PlayStations.

Nobody calls a hybrid automobile a Toyota. They call it a Prius.

Brands that get smothered.

There are exceptions. Many times, a corporate endorsement smothers the brand name, making it as useful as an appendix. Sony Bravia television sets and Sony Vaio computers, for example. Or Kodak EasyShare cameras.

How many consumers will say, "I bought a Bravia TV"? Almost none. The same is true of Vaio, an acronym for "video audio integrated operation," which also means nothing.

And how about Sharp Aquos television sets? Or Sharp Zaurus smartphones? Or Panasonic Viera HD television sets?

Every new category is an opportunity to build a new brand. Yet many companies miss out on these golden opportunities because they bury the new brand name with the better-known corporate name.

The first commercial digital camera was called the Sony Mavica. What was the role of that strange name, Mavica?

If Sony intended Mavica to become a brand name synonymous with digital cameras, then it should have launched the brand without the Sony name.

Try telling Sony management not to use the Sony name on its new digital camera and you can see what the problem is. Management falls in love with the company name and wants to make sure it's used everywhere. Especially when the new product is an important high-tech development.

It's corporate ego versus marketing principles, and guess who wins that battle?

Viera, Zaurus, Aquos, EasyShare, Vaio, and Bravia will someday join Mavica in history's wastepaper basket. Brand names that don't serve a real function ultimately become obsolete.

A new category needs a new brand name.

Right-brain marketing people know that, but left-brain management people do not.

A new brand name can often achieve strong perceptions that result in decades of profitable sales. Perceptions that include leadership and authenticity.

In some cases, the brand name can also become "generic" for the category.

- Silk for soy milk
- Scotch for cellophane tape
- Crocs for rubber sandals
- Softsoap for liquid soap
- Woolite for cold-water detergent
- Rollerblades for in-line skates

On the other hand, look at the digital-camera market. Kodak invented the digital camera. And Sony introduced the first commercial digital camera. Yet neither brand dominates the market. Here are market shares in a recent year.

- Canon: 20 percent
- Sony: 17 percent
- Kodak: 16 percent
- Nikon: 10 percent

Four brands, none of which are unique brands of digital cameras. They're all line extensions, either of film brands into the digital field or electronic brands into the camera field. It's not surprising that no single brand dominates the category.

Compare cameras with soft drinks. There are hundreds of companies marketing soft drinks in the United States, yet Gatorade has 82 percent of the sports-drink market. Coca-Cola has 60 percent of the cola market. Red Bull has 43 percent of the energy-drink market.

The first *new* brand into a new category usually ends up dominating that category, not the first brand into the new category, which often is a line extension of an existing brand. (Or a double-branded product like the Sony Mavica digital camera.)

Just being well known is not enough to make a great brand. What makes a great brand is dominating a market.

In the United States, Tabasco has 90 percent of the pepper-sauce market. Campbell's has 82 percent of the canned-soup market. Turbo Tax has 79 percent of the income-tax software market. Starbucks has 73 percent of the high-end coffeehouse market. The iPod has 70 percent of the MP3-player market. Taco Bell has 70 percent of the Mexican fast-food market. Google has 63 percent of the search market.

The subversive role of research.

You'll find very few Googles in the portfolios of Procter & Gamble, Unilever, Heinz, Kellogg, and General Mills. A shocking name like Google is not going to test very well.

Would you use a search site called Google, or would you prefer to use a search site with the Microsoft name? Before the launch of Google, there would have been no question which site consumers would have preferred.

In spite of the research, "known" names come with a lot of baggage. A known name already stands for something in the mind. In Microsoft's case, software. How can Microsoft also stand for search?

Companies often rationalize double branding by insisting that the brand is actually Whitestrips and Crest is the endorser. In a sense, that's true.

It's also the major reason for the recent rash of weak brand names. When you start with a strong brand name (Crest) and then try to combine it with another strong brand name, you have a problem.

Two strong brand names will fight each other. The only solution is to combine a strong brand name with a weak "generic-type" name. Crest with Whitestrips, for example.

Take Campbell Soup's portfolio of double brands.

- Campbell's Chunky
- Campbell's Soup at Hand
- Campbell's Select

Chunky, Soup at Hand, and Select are all trademarks of the Campbell Soup Company, but hardly strong brands.

They are no better, in our opinion, than descriptive words would have been: chunky, microwavable, and restaurant-style.

Campbell has taken the double-branding concept one step further. Now it is triple-branding some of its products.

- Campbell's Chunky Healthy Request
- Campbell's Select Healthy Request

(Here's a holistic idea for Campbell. Why not drop the Healthy Request brand and make all your soups healthy.)

Double branding in automobiles.

Nowhere is double branding more rampant. Yet some of the best automotive brands don't use double branding at all. They just use letters and numbers to differentiate their models. Lexus, BMW, Mercedes-Benz, Infiniti, and Volvo, for example. Some of their numbers actually make sense, as in the 1 series, 3 series, 5 series, and 7 series from BMW.

One double brander (Acura) found that its Legend model had higher name recognition than its master brand. So, for the 1996 model year, the Legend became the TL. In five years, Acura's name recognition went up 25 percent. Compared to 1996, Acura sales in 2007 were up 71 percent.

Double branding is like riding a teeter-totter. If one name goes up (Legend), the other name goes down (Acura.)

So which brand should an automobile manufacturer use? The answer is obvious. There are no Legend dealers; there are only Acura dealers.

Focus on the Acura name.

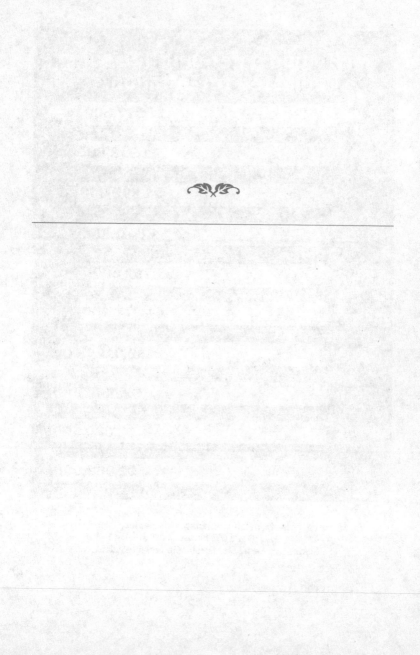

McDonald's per-unit U.S. sales adjusted for inflation.

Year	Sales
1998	$1,877,600
1999	$1,918,800
2000	$1,899,000
2001	$1,847,300
2002	$1,793,600
2003	$1,872,400
2004	$2,012,500
2005	$2,039,300
2006	$2,080,100
2007	$2,068,000

Adjusted for inflation, here are per-unit sales
of McDonald's restaurants in America.
In spite spending $6.7 billion on advertising in
the past ten years, sales remained relatively flat.

CHAPTER 15

Management plans on perpetual growth.
Marketing plans on market maturity.

"**W**e have to grow the business" is usually the first public statement of a new chief executive officer.

Growth solves all problems, goes the thinking. So the CEO sets the target for next year's sales increase—10 percent, 15 percent, 20 percent, depending on how aggressive the new chief executive is.

Even if a company misses its target, a "stretch goal" is considered to be a good thing.

A mathematical impossibility.

A stretch goal may not be such a good idea after all. Except for small gains made possible by increases in population and in the consumer price index, never-ending growth is mathematically impossible.

Twenty percent annual growth over a fifty-year period would mean that sales in the last year would be more than nine thousand times the initial period. While this might be possible for a start-up, it's impossible for any mature company.

The smallest *Fortune* 500 company is Scana of Columbia, South Carolina, which had sales in 2007 of $4.6 billion. If Scana grew 20 percent a year for fifty years, the company's sales in 2058 would be some $42 trillion (not including inflation), a figure which is about three times America's current gross domestic product.

Highly likely.

How can logical, analytical left-brain managers fail to see the consequences of perpetual growth? One possibility is that management is also short-term oriented. (See chapter 24.)

Sooner or later, a mature brand (not company, but brand) reaches an optimum point where further growth can only come from population growth and inflation. Recognizing this reality is the essence of good right-brain marketing thinking.

Muddling along at McDonald's.

Take McDonald's, for example. Per-unit restaurant sales in the United States have grown slowly in the past ten years, and because the market is saturated, the chain has not added many units.

1998: Units: 12,472. Sales per unit: $1,458,500.
1999: Units: 12,629. Sales per unit: $1,514,400.
2000: Units: 12,804. Sales per unit: $1,539,200.
2001: Units: 13,099. Sales per unit: $1,548,200.
2002: Units: 13,491. Sales per unit: $1,527,300.
2003: Units: 13,609. Sales per unit: $1,632,600.
2004: Units: 13,673. Sales per unit: $1,788,100.
2005: Units: 13,727. Sales per unit: $1,871,700.
2006: Units: 13,774. Sales per unit: $1,974,100.
2007: Units: 13,862. Sales per unit: $2,068,000.

In nine years, McDonald's average sales per restaurant unit increased 41.8 percent. Much of that growth was due to the rise in the consumer price index, which increased 29 percent in the same time period.

When you subtract the growth in the CPI from McDonald's actual growth, per-unit sales increases averaged about 1 percent a year. In other words, McDonald's has reached its maturity. At least in the U.S. market.

What has McDonald's management done in the past decade to try to "grow the business"? They have spent heavily on new menu items, new cooking equipment, and new promotions. All supported by massive consumer advertising programs.

Maybe, just maybe, a McDonald's restaurant of a given size and a given location has reached its optimum sales level of about $2 million per year. McDonald's has nothing to be ashamed of. In 2007, the average Burger King unit in the United States did only $1.24 million in sales.

What happens next?

Suppose this assumption is true. Suppose McDonald's has reached its optimum sales level. What are the implications for McDonald's marketing strategy?

McDonald's should reduce its menu options, reduce its advertising budget, and reduce the number of its consumer promotions. Instead of trying to increase sales per unit, McDonald's should try to maintain that $2 million per year per-unit average while reducing expenses and increasing profits.

Does that mean that the McDonald's Corporation should give up on growth? Not at all. It always has the option of introducing new brands that could go through the same cycle of (a) start-up, (b) accelerated growth, and (c) maturity.

Actually, McDonald's is doing the opposite. In 2006, it spun off Chipotle Mexican Grill. And the following year, it sold Boston Market to a private equity firm. Today, McDonald's Corporation is basically a hamburger chain.

Where would Procter & Gamble be today if it had stuck with soap?

Any company that has built a brand like McDonald's has a vast reservoir of systems, operating procedures, and marketing skills that could be used to launch second, third, and fourth brands. (One at a time, though.)

Nor is it clear that McDonald's menu expansion has necessarily been a good thing.

The incredible In-N-Out Burger.

Look at the success of a West Coast regional chain. In 2007, the average In-N-Out unit did $2,251,200 in sales. That was 9 percent higher than the average McDonald's unit.

The original McDonald's menu had three food items (hamburger, cheeseburger, and french fries), a malt shake, and five beverage items (coffee, Coca-Cola, milk, root beer, and orange drink.)

Today, a typical McDonald's might have some eighty items on its menu. And the company keeps on adding things, such as salads, chicken wraps, and espresso drinks.

From a logical left-brain point of view, the added items make sense. The obesity epidemic has created a market for healthier foods (let's add salads and chicken). The rise of Starbucks has created a market for high-end coffee drinks (let's add espresso.) As a matter of fact, everything added to a typical McDonald's menu makes management sense.

It just doesn't make marketing sense. If you want to build a dominant brand, you need to stand for something in the mind.

McDonald's used to stand for hamburgers. Today, it doesn't stand for much, yet its overwhelming retail presence and massive media expenditures keep the brand a leader in the fast-food game.

On the other hand, In-N-Out Burger has stuck awfully close to the original McDonald's concept. Today, In-N-Out has just four food items (hamburger, cheeseburger, double-double, and french fries), three flavors of shakes, and eight beverages.

The question is, what if McDonald's had also stuck with its original menu? Would the average McDonald's unit also have done $2,251,200 in sales last year?

We'll never know.

Growth is a marketing issue.

Management tends to push for growth at all costs. Yet there is a time to grow and a time to take your foot off the accelerator. And those decisions should be made from the brand's point of view, not from the company's point of view.

All companies have potential for growth. But not all brands do.

Now might be the time for McDonald's and other brands in similar situations to face that reality. And look for new opportunities.

Single-brand companies are particularly at risk from over-zealous management. Take Sony Corporation, for example.

In a recent survey of 5,000 U.S. consumers by AlixPartners, Sony was ranked as the most trusted brand, ahead of such well-known brands as Johnson & Johnson, Kraft, Toyota, Hewlett-Packard, Coca-Cola, Nike, and others.

In a recent survey of 3,600 Asian consumers by TNS, in collaboration with *Media* magazine, Sony was also ranked as the No. 1 brand.

As a brand, Sony is all-powerful. Yet as a company, Sony is a mess. In the past ten years, Sony has had sales of $658.3 billion and net profits after taxes of $12.1 billion, or a net profit margin of just 1.8 percent.

Compare Sony with the multibrand company Procter & Gamble. In the past ten years, Procter & Gamble has had sales of $537.3 billion and net profits after taxes of $64.6 billion, or a net profit margin of an astounding 12.0 percent.

Procter & Gamble is a smaller company than Sony, but a company that is making more than five times as much in net profits.

Red giants and white dwarfs.

Strong brand, strong sales, weak profits. Sony is not the only company that fits the "red giant" pattern.

Corporations are like stars. Toward the end of its life, a star the size of the Sun swells up into a red giant and becomes some one hundred times as large.

As a red giant exhausts its internal energy supplies, it loses its outer layers and finally shrinks to become a white dwarf, perhaps 1 percent of the diameter of the Sun.

Both Sony and General Motors are red giants. Sony, because

it puffed up its house brand. General Motors, because it puffed up each of its car brands until they didn't stand for anything.

Can either company escape the fate of all red giants, which eventually become white dwarfs? Only time will tell.

To escape its fate, Sony must shed many products and refocus on the segments in which it enjoys a leadership position. (The same strategy Jack Welch applied to General Electric: number one or number two, or forget about it.)

Management types have short memories. You might think the dismal performance of conglomerates in the 1960s and 1970s would have discouraged the recent trend toward "bulking up." But apparently not. Wherever you look, the emphasis is on growth.

Take Amazon.com and its original slogan, "Earth's biggest bookstore." Nice slogan and a nice analogy with the world's biggest river.

What is Amazon's current slogan? "Earth's biggest selection." Books have been shelved to make room for thirty-two other product lines, including Amazon's latest product introduction, food. (Shades of Webvan.)

In July 1995, Amazon opened its bookstore on the World Wide Web. In thirteen years, Amazon.com has sold $58.5 billion worth of merchandise. Not a bad haul. (Books, CDs, and DVDs still account for more than half of Amazon's sales.)

On the other hand, in those thirteen years of operation, Amazon.com has managed to lose $1.4 billion. How soon will Amazon.com break even? At current profit levels, it's going to take another three years.

Furthermore, all those additional products are slowing down the Web site for the majority of customers who just want to buy books. By some estimates, it takes five times as long to search for a given book title today as it did a decade ago.

What keeps red giants like Sony and Amazon.com in the ball game?

When you blow yourself up, everybody is impressed: customers, prospects, investors, and the media. You generate a lot of favorable publicity. (Think Donald Trump.) And you're able to sell a lot of stock to finance current operations.

The next red giant.

Another company that's in the early stages of turning itself into a red giant is Google. There's Google Maps (competing with MapQuest), Google Talk (competing with AIM and MSN Messenger), Google Finance (competing with Yahoo! Finance), Gmail (competing with Hotmail and Yahoo! e-mail), and Google Checkout (competing with PayPal). Then there's Google software for personal computers and cell phones.

Google is also planning to extend its brand into targeted advertising for radio, television, and newspapers.

"Google. So much fanfare, so few hits" was the headline of a recent article in *BusinessWeek*. "An analysis of some two dozen new ventures launched over the past four years shows that Google has yet to establish a single market leader outside its core search business," the publication concluded.

In addition to being relatively unsuccessful, all of these line extensions are diluting the power of the Google brand. In the long run, Google's stranglehold on the search market is in danger, but not from its traditional competitors, Yahoo! and MSN, because these brands are even more "unfocused" than Google.

The danger comes from new brands with a single-minded search focus and which offer something totally different from the Google formula. One potential winner is Cuil, an old Irish name pronounced like "cool."

At Cuil.com, search results are presented in an attractive magazine format, including pictures.

Profit seems to be a dirty word today.

Too many companies are focused on the top rather than on the bottom line. Red giants like General Motors and Sony have revenues that exceed the gross domestic product of many small countries.

Growth is the mantra for many CEOs. Get big in a hurry, and then look for ways to make money.

Yet nature offers many examples of the superiority of slow, not rapid, growth. Slow-growing hardwood trees outlive fast-growing softwood trees.

Rapid growth weakens rather than strengthens. That's true for a brand as well as for a plant.

One of the strongest companies (and strongest brands) is Nintendo, a company that just markets video games and consoles. Between fiscal 2000 and fiscal 2006, Nintendo sales actually fell from $5.3 billion to $4.3 billion, a decline of 19 percent.

Yet Nintendo made more money in fiscal 2006 ($836.6 million) than it did in fiscal 2000 ($531.3 million.) Furthermore, Nintendo's profit margins are remarkable. In the past ten years, Nintendo's net profits after taxes were 15.5 percent of sales.

Eat your heart out, Sony.

Zinc-carbon.

Alkaline.

Lithium.

Eveready pioneered the zinc-carbon battery.
Duracell pioneered the alkaline battery.
There's an opportunity to build a lithium brand,
but so far the category has only line extensions.

CHAPTER 16

Management tends to kill new categories. Marketing tends to build new categories.

It's not deliberate, but many left-brain management people favor policies that tend to kill emerging new categories.

Right-brain marketing people, on the other hand, tend to favor policies that build new categories.

It can cost a fortune for a company to pioneer a new category of product or service. Digital cameras, for example. Or satellite radio. Or Internet grocery service. Webvan, for example, lost $830 million on its two-year venture into the grocery-delivery business.

Since it's so costly to establish a new category, why would any company deliberately want to kill an emerging new category?

Two kinds of companies.

Actually there are good reasons for putting the kibosh on a new category. In the business jungle, there are category builders and category killers.

A category builder is often a start-up or a small company

that hopes to compete with a bigger company by introducing a new brand that defines an emerging new category.

Invariably, these small companies are run by right-brain entrepreneurs who have marketing instincts. (Think Charles Schwab, the first discount broker. Kevin Plank of Under Armour, the first athletic underwear. Larry Ellison of Oracle, the first relational database software company.)

A small company with good marketing instincts, for example, introduced Duracell, an alkaline battery that lasts twice as long as the zinc-carbon batteries made by Eveready, the leading battery brand.

A unit of the much larger Union Carbide company, Eveready was run by category killers. Six years prior to Duracell's launch, Eveready introduced its own alkaline battery. It called the new product (naturally) the Eveready alkaline battery.

Eveready management had hoped that "appliance battery" would remain a single category with various "choices," such as zinc carbon, alkaline, and so on. As the leading appliance-battery brand, Eveready would then be able to dominate the category for decades to come.

A win for the category builder.

It never happened. Thanks to the marketing skill put behind the Duracell brand, consumers eventually perceived that there were two categories of appliance batteries: inexpensive zinc-carbon batteries and long-lasting alkaline batteries. Today, those two categories are represented by two brands: Eveready and Duracell.

Eveready management finally realized it couldn't kill the alkaline category, so it launched Energizer, its own brand of alkaline battery. But like many left-brain management moves, it was too late in the game.

Money cannot make up for lost time. In spite of massive advertising investments, Energizer remains No.2 behind the dominant Duracell brand.

Creativity cannot make up for lost time, either. *Advertising Age* named the pink drum-playing Energizer bunny as one of the 10 best advertising icons of the 20th century (No. 5).

The second-generation campaign, which showed the Energizer bunny interrupting ads for fictional products, was cited by *Advertising Age* as one of the 100 best advertising campaigns of the twentieth century (No. 34).

Meanwhile, Duracell was turning itself into a company run by management types. It was first purchased by Dart, then Kraft, then Kohlberg Kravis Roberts, then Gillette, and currently, Procter & Gamble.

At each stage of the game, Duracell was bought by a larger, more managerial-type company.

A win for the category killers.

Today, both big battery brands are run by big-company management types who have apparently succeeded in killing the next generation battery: lithium.

There's no question that "lithium" could have been perceived as a separate category. But for that to happen, the lithium category would have needed a separate brand name synonymous with the category. (As Thomas' is with English muffins. Or Pop-Tarts with toaster pastry. Or A1 with steak sauce.)

In marketing, timing is everything. Once a category is dead, it remains dead.

Both Duracell-branded and Energizer-branded lithium batteries have been on the market for quite some time. It's too late for a marketing-oriented category builder to get into the lithium game.

And so it goes. Sometimes the category builders win. Sometimes the category killers win.

Why are many opportunities missed?

No one can see the future. In the early stages, it isn't always clear whether a new concept will develop into a separate category.

In the early stages of the World Wide Web, it wasn't obvious that the Internet would become a new media category. And not only a new category, but one that would become more important than all the traditional media combined: books, newspapers, magazines, radio, and television.

You sometimes get the feeling that management people believe that new categories are created by God. And that new categories won't arrive until the time is right, all dictated by some higher power.

Marketing people believe otherwise. They realize that a company's marketing activities can create a new category that can benefit the category builder. As the alkaline category benefited the Duracell brand.

A loss for a category builder.

What's the largest-selling beer in America? Budweiser, with some $8 billion in annual sales.

It could have been otherwise. Miller Brewing missed the chance of a lifetime to overtake Budweiser. What Duracell achieved in alkaline batteries, Miller Brewing was unable to achieve in light beer.

Miller's mistake? To launch the first light beer, the brewer picked a bad name: Lite.

Lite, a bad brand name for a light beer? You can see how logical-thinking management can get confused. Why in the world would Lite be a bad name for a light beer?

Generic names such as Lite are bad brand names because competitors can destroy their uniqueness by launching similar brands. Schlitz Light. Pabst Light. Coors Light. Natural Light. Bud Light.

Miller's instincts, however, were sound. They tried to build a new category by leaving the Miller name off the new brand and just calling it Lite. But they had to back off when they couldn't protect their Lite trademark against the "light" beers introduced by a raft of category killers.

And so Lite beer became Miller Lite. And the battle to build a new category was lost. Too bad for Miller Brewing.

Today, light beer greatly outsells regular beer. (Bud Light, the largest-selling beer, has annual U.S. sales of about $4.7 billion. The number two brand, Budweiser regular, has about $2.8 billion.)

Who wins when a new category dies?

The market leader of the existing category, of course. Even though Anheuser-Busch was virtually the last major brewer to introduce a light beer, Bud Light is now the number one brand.

Today, light beer is not perceived as a new category. Light beer is perceived as regular beer, just watered down a bit.

That's why Budweiser won the light-beer war, and that's why Duracell will win the lithium-battery war. If you want to kill an emerging new category, first make sure your brand is the leading brand of the existing category.

Diet cola was a replay of the light-beer story. The first brand of diet cola was Diet Rite, a bad name and, even worse, a generic name.

(Would Microbrewed Rite have become a successful beer brand like Samuel Adams? Of course not.)

Diet Rite cola is almost as generic as Lite beer. So the emerging new category was easy pickings for the category killers, Pepsi-Cola and Coca-Cola. First in the pool was Diet Pepsi, followed by Diet Coke.

Today, diet cola is not perceived as a new category. Diet cola is perceived as regular cola with the sugar replaced by an artificial sweetener.

And the leading diet cola is Diet Coke, the last brand into the diet pool, but the leader of the existing category.

Microbrew vs. light beer.

Take "microbrew" beer, a new category built by Jim Koch with his launch of Samuel Adams Boston Lager. Ironically, the beer was initially brewed in Pittsburgh by the folks who produce Iron City beer.

No matter. "Microbrew" made it into the beer drinker's mind as the name of a new type of beer. Both Anheuser-Busch and Miller Brewing struck back with their own specialty beers (Anheuser World Select and Miller Reserve, for example).

But they were unable to kill the emerging microbrew category. Today, Samuel Adams, the category builder, is a big winner.

There's no logical reason why beer brewed in small batches (microbrew) should be perceived as a separate category and beer brewed with substantially fewer calories (light) should not.

Of the two concepts, a "light" beer is a more radical development than a "small-batch" beer. A beer drinker is more likely to notice the difference between a light and a regular beer than between a small-batch and a big-batch beer.

The difference is not in the beer; it's in the marketing.

The biggest mistake of logical management types is their failure to see the rise of a new category. They seem to believe that categories are firmly fixed and a new one seldom arises, except by a truly revolutionary development.

Furthermore, when a company owns a category, its management tends to see new developments as just "improvements" in an existing category, not as opportunities to create new categories by launching new brands.

Pigeons and pigeonholes.

One useful analogy is to visualize the mind as a pigeon coop. The pigeonholes are the categories and the pigeons are the brands.

Not every hole is filled with a pigeon, of course. "High-priced Korean cars" is a logical category, but there are no high-priced Korean car brands.

Except that Hyundai has just introduced the $40,000 Hyundai Genesis.

That's a typical left-brain management mistake. Trying to fit one pigeon into two pigeonholes. The consumer likes to keep things simple.

Is Hyundai a cheap car or an expensive car? If it's a cheap car, it won't fit into the expensive-car pigeonhole.

If it's an expensive car, it won't fit into the inexpensive-car pigeonhole.

In labeling a new pigeonhole, consumers are particularly sensitive to price levels. In general, every category is really three distinctive categories: high price, low price, and mid-range price.

In vodka, for example, Grey Goose is a high-price pigeon. Smirnoff is a low-price pigeon and Absolut is a midrange pigeon.

In restaurant chains, Ruth's Chris is a high-price pigeon. McDonald's is a low-price pigeon and Olive Garden is a mid-range pigeon.

In bottled water, Evian is a high-price pigeon. Aquafina is a low-price pigeon and Poland Spring is a midrange pigeon.

"It's only a name" is a management refrain heard repeatedly in the boardroom. Yet the name is crucial to the strategy of creating a new pigeonhole.

What creates a new category anyway? Forget reality. It's perceptions in the minds of consumers.

If consumers believe it's a new category, it's a new category.

New pigeonholes take time to build.

It can take an exceptionally long time to build a new category. Tylenol, for example, was introduced in 1956 as a prescription brand of acetaminophen. Four years later, the brand went over-the-counter.

Eight years after hitting the drugstores, Tylenol sales were still a meager $5 million a year. In 1975 (nineteen years after its introduction), the first Tylenol consumer advertising ran.

Today, Tylenol is the largest-selling brand in American drugstores.

Slow growth tends to tranquilize the competition. It was many years before Bayer responded with advertisements like these:

- "Makers of Tylenol, shame on you!"
- "No. Tylenol is <u>not</u> found safer than Aspirin."

The ads were signed "Bayer ASPIRIN." This was a major mistake. If you want to kill an emerging category, you don't emphasize your existing category. You need to broaden your category to encompass the new one.

"Bayer pain reliever" would have been a much better signature for the ads.

Organic: category or not?

So far no category builder, with the exception of Whole Foods and Horizon milk, has been able to accomplish much of anything in the organic category.

There are a host of organic category killers at work. Walk the aisles of any supermarket and you'll see dozens of examples. Del Monte canned peas and Del Monte organic canned peas, for instance.

With all the publicity "low carb" received, it never became a category—for the same reason. Almost every packaged-goods maker jumped into low carb with their line-extended brands, effectively smothering the opportunity to create a separate category.

The classic mistake of a potential category builder is to try to do too much. Launching a broad line of products under a single brand name, for example.

Healthy Choice made this mistake by introducing hundreds

of products under that brand name. Few consumers today consider "healthy" as a category. Rather, they see Healthy Choice as just another brand name.

It's much better to start narrow and then broaden the line only after it has won its category-builder battle. Horizon started with organic milk and then broadened its line to include other milk-based products: butter, cheese, sour cream, yogurt, etc.

Another mistake is waiting too long. Will premium coffee at McDonald's kill the category Starbucks has so skillfully built? We think not. It's too late.

Smirnoff also waited too long to try to kill the premium vodka category built by Absolut. Smirnoff Black never went anywhere as a brand or as a category killer.

When Grey Goose came along, the vodka competitors didn't even try. Instead, they launched their own ultra-premium brands. Level by Absolut. Elit by Stolichnaya.

And who will win this battle? Silly question.

Grey Goose.

Again, once consumers are convinced a new category exists, the first brand into the mind always wins.

Most consumers have a strong preference for Heinz
instead of Hunt's, the number two ketchup brand.
Yet they cannot articulate a single reason why.
Heinz "owns" the ketchup position in the mind.

CHAPTER 17

Management wants to communicate.
Marketing wants to position.

In the context of marketing, what is communications anyway? It's a message sent by a company via a medium to a group of prospects.

Let's say you read a newspaper this morning. In that newspaper were hundreds of advertisements with hundreds of pictures and thousands of words. Now suppose there was a service that could measure your mind to find how many of those words or ideas or concepts or pictures wound up there.

They would find very few.

In 2007, the three largest advertised brands in America were AT&T, Verizon, and Sprint.

AT&T spent $2.2 billion. Verizon spent $2.1. billion. And Sprint spent $1.2 billion. That's a total of $5.5 billion, or the equivalent of $18.15 for every person in America.

What's the difference?

For all that money, what's an AT&T? What's a Verizon? What's a Sprint? We don't know, do you?

- What's the difference between Crest and Colgate toothpaste?
- Between Duracell and Energizer batteries?
- Between Visa and MasterCard?
- Between Aquafina and Dasani water?

In spite of the fact that we are bombarded daily with massive amounts of advertising, most of us know little about the brands we buy. How they are made. Where they are made. What ingredients they contain. Why they are better (or different) than other brands.

It's not that companies haven't tried to communicate these facts. Total advertising expenditures in a recent year have been estimated at $290 billion, or $960 per person. (About twice as much as the country is spending on the war in Iraq.)

Renegade, fearless, unexpected, and so on.

Take a five-page foldout magazine advertisement that opened up with the following thirty-nine attributes spread out over two pages: renegade, fearless, unexpected, bold, true, spontaneous, curious, intriguing, unwavering, rare, brash, provocative, intuitive, genuine, daring, uncommon, irreverent, brazen, absolute, unusual, visionary, idyllic, proud, maverick, wild, undaunted, resolute, poetic, dynamic, soulful, unconventional, strong, romantic, authentic, brave, unorthodox, deft, radical, and dreamer.

What brand could possibly combine all these wonderful things? Turn the page and you get the answer: the new 315-horsepower FX45. And who makes the wonderful, new 315-horsepower FX45?

There, in small type at the bottom of the next page, is the answer: "Infiniti, accelerating the future."

What's wrong with this advertisement? And thousands more just like it? They assume that the primary function of advertising is to communicate. "Tell more, sell more" was the old advertising adage.

Advertising is not communications; advertising is positioning. The best advertising communicates precious little about the brand.

What the best advertising does, however, is to establish and reinforce a position in the prospect's mind.

What's an Infiniti? We don't know, do you? What we do know is that an Infiniti is not a "renegade, fearless, unexpected" automobile.

An Infiniti is a Japanese automobile with a big problem called Lexus.

What's a Rolex?

You don't have to communicate much of anything to build a great brand. What do you know about Rolex except that it's an expensive Swiss watch?

The "best" expensive Swiss watch.

Do you know where Rolexes are made? How they are made? What makes them different from less-expensive Swiss watches? As a matter of fact, do you know anything about Rolex except that it's the best expensive Swiss watch?

Probably not. Nor do you need to know much more than that. That's the Rolex position.

A mind is too small a container to hold all the marketing messages companies are trying to stuff into it. Trying to communicate more information than is absolutely necessary is self-defeating. It can actually reduce the effectiveness of a marketing program. It can also reduce the mystique of the brand.

The primary function of a marketing organization is to position the brand. That's the goal that should always be kept in mind.

It can be shocking to learn how little information the average prospect holds in his or her mind. Take the late Peter Drucker, for example.

To management people, Peter Drucker was the "ultimate" management guru.

But what do you know about his principles? What did he have to say about managing a business?

"Aaaah . . . he was a guru," the average company executive might say. And what else does that person need to know to hold Peter Drucker in an exalted position in the mind? Nothing.

Waiting in the wings to take Peter Drucker's place is Ram Charan, coauthor of *Execution: The Discipline of Getting Things Done* and the recipient of recent favorable articles in *Fortune* and *BusinessWeek*.

The passing of Peter Drucker leaves an open hole in the mind for the next "ultimate management guru." And, sure enough, there was a candidate waiting to take his place.

Knowing too much can hurt the process.

Politicians have learned this principle. If a politician takes a position on every issue in an election, he or she is bound to offend everybody. And possibly lose everybody's vote.

Hillary Clinton's problem was that voters knew too much about her. Whereas Barack Obama was an empty slate.

When a politician is an empty slate, voters can project their own positive attributes on the candidate as long as he or she "looks and acts the part."

Furthermore, Barack Obama made the exceedingly wise decision to focus his entire campaign on a single word: change. While the other candidates tried to communicate a wide range of ideas and concepts, Obama positioned himself as the agent of "change."

Change worked against Hillary Clinton who was perceived as a longtime Washington insider. And change worked against John McCain who was perceived as another Republican politician.

"Better ingredients, better pizza," says Papa John's. As a result of its brilliant positioning, Papa John's has become the third-largest pizza chain in America and one of the fastest growing.

Do you know what the better ingredients are? Do you know that Papa John's uses fresh crushed tomatoes, real mozzarella cheese, and distilled water in the preparation of the dough? Most people don't.

Does it matter? Probably not. "Better ingredients, better pizza" is enough to position Papa John's a step above Pizza Hut and Domino's.

It's important to note that Papa John's was not successful because it made better pizzas than its competitors. (This may or may not be true.) Papa John's was successful because it created the perception that it made better pizza than its mainstream competitors.

That's not an easy task. Too many management types think that a better product automatically creates a better perception. It doesn't usually happen.

What created a better perception for Papa John's was the skillful use of a positioning strategy to induce consumers to put the brand in their minds as a "step above" the other pizzas.

If you study advertising messages, you'll find that most brands "claim" to be better than their competition. But most brands fail to position themselves as better.

Are we trying to communicate or position?

That's the question that every company should ask itself before starting a marketing program.

Look at the automobile communications problem, not from the point of view of the communicator, but from the point of view of the communicatee.

There are hundreds of car models. The 2008 Buying Guide of *Consumer Reports* reviewed 240 different car models and gives individual ratings for seventeen different "trouble spots" for each of six different model years.

How many consumers are going to pay attention to this wealth of detail? Very few. Most consumers have their hearts set on one or two specific brands.

They go down to the dealer, kick the tires, sit behind the wheel, look for the cup holders, stretch their feet in the backseat, and somehow make up their mind which one to buy.

As a matter of fact, can you even position a car model like the FX45? For the most part, the answer is no. There are just too many individual car models to conveniently fit into the average mind.

The best you can do is to position the car brand. And only a handful of car brands have done so. Lexus is the *luxury* Japanese car, but what word does Infiniti own? Or what word do they want to own? Or what word can they own?

These are the questions the left-brain leaders at Infiniti should be asking themselves.

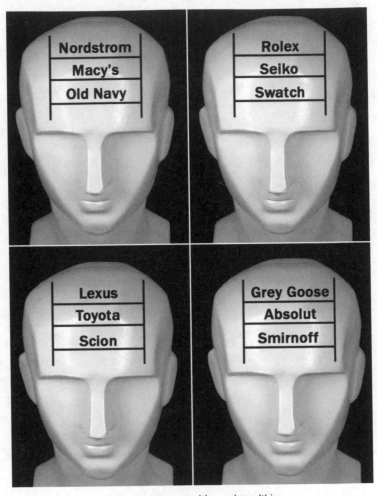

As consumers get older and wealthier,
they change brands to reflect their new status.
Instead of chasing customers "up the ladder,"
a company should just let them go.

CHAPTER 18

Management wants customers for life. Marketing is happy with a short-term fling.

Management is greedy. It wants to create customers for life. As a matter of fact, a typical question a management type might ask of its marketing department is: "What's the lifetime value of our average customer?"

Presumably, a company benefits by keeping its customers satisfied over an extended period of time.

Nice idea in theory, but this kind of thinking often leads a company down the wrong path.

The ultimate in customer satisfaction.

That was Saturn's strategy. Comfortable showrooms, no high-pressure salespeople, no haggling over price. "A different kind of company. A different kind of car."

The first Saturn model, the S series, was wildly successful. But what would happen when a Saturn customer got older and made more money?

No problem, decided Saturn management. They'd take care of their customers by introducing the L series, a larger, more-expensive model. "The next big thing from Saturn." (What could be more logical?)

Not a good move. Sales of the S series fell because the model was "long in the tooth." Sales of the L series suffered because consumers thought "it was a little too expensive for a Saturn."

Saturn was a great car for young, single people just getting started in life. But what happens when you grow up, get promoted, and make more money? Do you want to buy a more-expensive Saturn?

Most young people we know would rather have a BMW. When you move up the ladder of life, you want your brand to reflect your new status.

What happens when you get married and have kids? Do you want to pile the family into a Saturn SUV?

Most young people we know would rather have a Volvo, the car that says you care about your family's safety.

Then, in the normal course of events, you get divorced. What happens next? The wife keeps the kids and the Volvo, and the husband buys a Ferrari.

Let your customers go.

Instead of constantly staking out new ground, you can usually build a better brand if you constantly fertilize the plot you already own. Let your customers move up the ladder.

What happens in cars also happens in clothing, cosmetics, beer, liquor, watches, and many other consumer products. Consumers know they are getting ahead in life when they can leave their old brands behind.

When you were a child, a trip to McDonald's was probably the high point of your day. As a teenager, however, you probably hung out at Wendy's. After college, you might have moved up to Outback Steakhouse. After you get promoted, you might have celebrated with your date at Ruth's Chris.

Then, in the normal course of events, you got married and had kids and got dragged right back to McDonald's.

A teenager might buy a Swatch to wear to high school, then a Seiko to take to college, and at graduation might have received a Rolex.

Brands are the markers on the rungs of the ladder of life. As you move up the ladder, you measure your progress by changing your brands.

A young woman might buy her clothing at The Gap. As she gets older, she moves up to Macy's. As her fortunes increase, she moves on to Nordstrom.

Young people drink beer; older people drink wine. Beer is inexpensive, so it has become the alcoholic beverage of choice for the younger crowd.

But that identification with youth motivates the older person to switch to wine. In a fine restaurant, many older people would be embarrassed to order beer.

Beer is at the bottom of the alcohol ladder and wine is at the top. That's why expensive beer doesn't sell particularly well. Neither does cheap wine.

Brands define who we are.

We select our brands based on their positions in our minds and whether they match how we feel about ourselves. When a brand no longer stands for something, it loses its power.

In some cases, it would pay a company to actively discourage consumers to grow old with its brand.

One brand in trouble is Levi's. The company peaked in 1996 with revenues of $7.1 billion. Since then, it has generally gone downhill, with 2007 revenues of just $4.3 billion.

One of Levi Strauss's problems is that older people wear the brand. No kid wants to wear what their parents wear.

We would have restricted Levi's jeans to waist sizes no larger than thirty-two inches.

Let those big old butts walk around wearing Wranglers.

Introducing Starbucks
PIKE PLACE ROAST

Come try our new daily brew,
Pike Place Roast, on us. It's
roasted fresh, ground fresh
and brewed fresh every day.

STARBUCKS · FRESH ROASTED COFFEE ®

When the Starbucks chain got into trouble,
they distributed a "Brewed Coffee Card,"
good for one free twelve-ounce cup of coffee
every Wednesday for eight weeks in a row.

CHAPTER 19

Management loves coupons and sales.
Marketing loathes them.

Macy's, the 825-unit department-store chain, had a great idea: cut back on coupons and lure consumers with exclusive merchandise from fashion houses like Martha Stewart and Oscar de la Renta.

It didn't work. "Given fewer coupons to clip," reported the *New York Times,* "bargain hunters snub Macy's."

So Macy's did a U-turn and went back to its decades-old strategy of carpet-bombing consumers with coupons, coupons, coupons.

And management types around the country said, "See, we told you so. Coupons are the lifeblood of retailing today."

Why the addiction to coupons?

For short-term, bottom-line, rational thinkers, coupons are a no-brainer. A company knows exactly how much money it spent on its coupon activities and also how many coupons arrived in the cash registers of its retailers.

A few simple mathematical calculations and the company

can determine the return on its coupon investment. No wonder they are extremely popular.

In a recent year, according to NCH, a coupon-processing company, consumer packaged-goods companies distributed some 279 billion coupons That's about 2,600 coupons per household.

According to another source, the top twenty manufacturers, including Procter & Gamble and General Mills, account for about 60 percent of all coupons issued. (That's not surprising. It's the big companies that distribute most of the coupons.)

That's packaged goods only. It does not count the billions of coupons distributed by national retail chains, local stores, restaurants, and other outlets.

For marketing types, coupons are not what they seem to be. Couponing is a marketing activity that's almost impossible to measure.

It's easy, of course, to count the coupons in a cash register. But it's not possible to count the customers who would have bought anyway, with or without a coupon.

Nor is it possible to count the prospects who didn't buy because they didn't have a current coupon. Nor is it possible to measure the damage to the brand because of the price-cutting activity created by the coupons.

And as Macy's found out, it's difficult to break the habit once you start down the coupon road.

Cigarettes, crack cocaine, and coupons.

All three are addictions. No smoker in his or her right mind would continue smoking (or even have taken up cigarettes in the first place) if the cigarettes themselves weren't addictive. Why make the same mistake with coupons?

Marketing success and couponing are inversely correlated. The more a store or a chain uses coupons, the less successful that store or chain is likely to be.

Successful chains like Starbucks seldom issue coupons. Instead, they issue what might be "anticoupons." For example, you buy a Starbucks card for $15 to $100, and the company puts the money in the bank and collects interest until you get ready to order your regular grande caffe latte.

Left-brain management considers coupons a strategy. Right-brain marketing considers coupons a crutch. They might be able to keep your business alive until you can figure out what your real strategy ought to be.

Coupons are not cheap, either. Sunday freestanding inserts have about a 1 percent redemption rate and a $10 cost per thousand. That means each coupon redeemed has cost the company $1 plus the face value of the coupon itself plus the processing costs.

The houseware-chain war.

A coupon war is like a real war. When the conflict ends, both sides are usually worse off.

Coupons might be a lousy strategy, but they might be a necessity for a company under attack. In much the same way, it wouldn't make sense for a country to start a nuclear war. But if a country was under attack, it might be the only sensible response.

Over the years, the war between the two major houseware chains, Bed Bath & Beyond and Linens 'n Things, has been fought with "20 percent off" coupons. Month after month, both chains shower consumers with their 20 percent discount offers. Only a spendthrift would shop at one of those chains without a coupon in hand.

In spite of the coupons, the leader in the category (Bed Bath & Beyond) is doing well. In the last four years, revenues have been increasing about 14 percent per year, and net profit margins, on average, have been 9.4 percent.

The number two chain, Linens 'n Things, is not doing nearly as well. After slumping sales, the company put itself up for sale and was acquired by a private equity firm in 2005. And recently, Linens 'n Things filed for bankruptcy protection and is closing all of its stores.

We have no way of knowing, but our feeling is that Linens 'n Things started the coupon war and Bed Bath & Beyond retaliated. Bad strategy for an also-ran. Necessary strategy for a leader brand.

Coupons do only half the damage inflicted on consumer brands. The other half is inflicted by sales.

Black Friday.

The day after Thanksgiving, America's retail chains organize a shopping orgy.

Opening early, many retailers compete to see which chain can offer the deepest discounts. In a recent year, The Sports Authority offered "6-hour doorbusters," from 5:30 a.m. to 11:30 a.m. Twenty-five percent off the entire stock.

Toys "R" Us offered "Lowest prices ever," 50 percent off and more from 5:00 a.m. to noon.

Sears offered "Insanely early Friday Specials" from 5:00 a.m. to 11:00 a.m. The first two hundred customers in each store got a free $10 reward card.

At Pep Boys, from 6:00 a.m. to 11:00 a.m., the first fifty customers got a free $10 shopping card.

Some of the promotions were exceedingly complicated. At

Ashley Furniture Homestore, it was 20 percent off from 7:00 a.m. to 9:00 a.m., 15 percent off from 9:00 a.m. to 11:00 a.m., 10 percent off from 11:00 a.m. to 1:00 p.m., and 5 percent off from 1:00 p.m. to closing time.

The shopping orgy was Friday, but the advertising orgy was Thursday. In Atlanta, for example, the local newspaper (the *Atlanta Journal-Constitution*) carried 385 display ads (not including house ads) in addition to forty inserts with 358 pages of advertising.

America's retailers paid handsomely for the privilege of offering consumers those deep discounts.

Newton's third law states, "For every action, there is an equal and opposite reaction." What is the opposite reaction when a chain offers to sell its wares at deep discounts?

"Your regular prices are too high."

Unfortunately for retailers, that's the opposite reaction as far as consumers are concerned.

Is that what most retailers want to communicate? We think not. Most retailers want to communicate the fact that their retail outlets feature great merchandise at reasonable prices. Or as Macy's used to say, "It's smart to be thrifty."

Coupons, sales, special discounts for customers using membership cards, and a host of price promotions have steadily undermined the idea that any particular chain is a good place to shop . . . unless there is a sale.

Store sales are like crack cocaine. You get a short-term high followed by a long-term low. The only way to get high again is to have another sale.

The Circuit City customer who bought a thirty-two-inch

HD LCD television set for $499.99 on Friday isn't going to buy another one on Monday at the full price of $899.99. Furthermore, he or she is going to be leery of buying any major appliance at Circuit City unless there's a sale going on.

Where is the discount derby headed? If history is any guide, it's headed in the same direction as the airline industry. It was the airline industry that perfected the high-low approach to marketing. High prices for consumers who have no other choice. Low prices for consumers who could find cheap fares on other airlines.

What happened in the airline industry can also happen in retail generally. As the Syms slogan says, "An educated consumer is our best customer." As consumers get educated about retailers' high-low strategies, they tend to move to chains that feature "everyday low prices."

In the airline industry, it was the "no-frills" airlines with their everyday low prices that undermined the high-low strategies of the major carriers.

Warren Buffett famously remarked that if there were a capitalist present at Kitty Hawk in 1903, he should have shot Orville Wright down. It would have saved his progeny money.

We disagree. There are no bad businesses; there are only bad business strategies.

In the last ten years, Southwest Airlines had a net profit margin of 7.3 percent. By comparison, the average *Fortune* 500 company had a net profit margin in the same period of just 5.5 percent.

All sale, no branding.

What's tragic about the retail industry's "sale" mentality is the almost complete absence of branding in their marketing efforts.

We leafed through the 358 pages of insert advertising in a recent Thanksgiving issue of the *Atlanta Journal-Constitution,* and it was hard to find any mention of what any individual store stood for. Nothing but sale, sale, sale.

Many chains today do almost no advertising except sale advertising. The furniture industry is famous for its "all-sale, all-the-time" approach.

Another heavy advertiser that does nothing but sale advertising is Jos. A. Bank. Its Web site sets the pattern.

- Entire stock of top coats. 60% off.
- All pinpoint dress shirts. Now $29. Reg. $59.50.
- Entire stock of pattern sport coats. 60% off.

You can bet on it. The day a chain starts down the continuous-sale path is the day the chain is headed for trouble.

Strong brands do little sale advertising. We have never seen a Starbucks advertisement offering two cappuccinos for the price of one.

Nor have we seen an Apple advertisement offering an iPod for 50 percent off. Or a Rolex advertisement offering two watches for the price of one.

On Thanksgiving Day, when all the other retailers were running their sale, sale, sale advertisements, Whole Foods ran an ad in the Atlanta newspapers with the headline: "Today we give thanks to all our local growers."

That's class. That's a great brand.

By being the opposite of Red Bull in the U.S.,
Monster became the number two energy drink.
Red Bull was introduced in an 8.3-ounce can,
Monster in a 16-ounce monstersize can.

CHAPTER 20

Management tries to copy the competition.
Marketing tries to be the opposite.

You know the kids' game. Rock (fist) breaks scissors. Scissors (two fingers) cuts paper. Paper (flat hand) covers rock.

So what's the best strategy in a game of rock/ paper/ scissors? The answer is obvious. It all depends on what strategy the other kid is using.

So, too, in marketing. Your best strategy often depends on what strategy your competitors are using.

Management seldom sees it this way. Logically, there can be only one "best" strategy. "So what if our competitors are also using the same strategy," thinks management. "Do we want to go with less-than-the-best strategy?"

"Furthermore, our competitors are smart, too. They must know what they're doing."

"We'll just use the same strategy and then do it better than the competition."

There's logic to management's thinking. "Even if our competitors are wrong, we'll still win by doing the wrong thing, only better."

It's the same strategy used by the leading boat in a yacht race. "Tack when the number two boat tacks. That way we'll stay in front no matter what."

Marketing looks at the situation differently. Instead of copying the competition, a marketing person looks for an opportunity to be the opposite.

Coca-Cola is widely perceived to the real thing, the authentic brand, the longtime market leader. So how does Pepsi-Cola become the opposite of the real thing?

Coca-Cola is a brand that has been around for a long time. (More than 120 years.) It's the cola your parents drank.

"The Pepsi Generation."

So Pepsi-Cola became the opposite. The cola for the younger crowd. *Advertising Age* selected the Pepsi marketing program as one of the one hundred best advertising campaigns of the twentieth century (No. 21).

Over the years, "The Pepsi Generation" is the only marketing strategy that has substantially moved the needle for the number two cola.

In case you haven't noticed, it's been decades since the Pepsi Generation has been seen on television. Why? Because logic took over.

"The one drawback of Pepsi advertising in the past has been a little too much focus on youth," said Phil Dusenberry, vice chairman at Pepsi's advertising agency, BBDO. "We could have made greater gains had we expanded our horizons to cast a wider net and catch more people rather than kids only."

Who could argue with the logic of appealing to everyone instead of just appealing to the younger generation? The flaw in the logic lies in the mind of the consumer.

A product that appeals to everyone has no unique identity. It doesn't stand for anything different. It's just another cola, only better.

Pepsi's current campaign reflects this lack of identity. "It's the cola" is a typical left-brain management approach: "We've got the better product, our research shows we've got the better product, and, by God, we're going to do our best to convince consumers of this fact."

What the management at Pepsi and other companies often forget is that a narrow approach to the mind doesn't necessarily mean a narrow approach to the market.

Cola is a young person's drink that on many occasions adults also consume. Establishing your cola brand as the "with-it" product for the younger generation also appeals to older people who want to "think young."

Management tends to be "inner-directed." What are we? What do we want to be? How do we get to where we want to be? CEOs often brag about doing their own thing and ignoring the competition.

Marketing tends to be "other-directed." Who's the leader in the category? If it's not us, then how do we become the opposite of the brand that is the leader?

Years ago, we tried to get Burger King to become the opposite of McDonald's with absolutely no success.

What's a McDonald's in the American market? It's a place for the younger crowd, especially kids between the ages of two and six. They drag their parents to McDonald's, attracted by the Ronald McDonald character, the happy meals, and the swings and slides.

"Grow up, kid, to flame broiling."

That was the slogan we presented to Burger King. The idea was to position the brand as the place for older kids who had outgrown the happy meals.

Instead, Burger King tried to outdo McDonald's. Bigger playgrounds and better kids' meals were just some of the "better-than" strategies they employed. Needless to say, the "better-than" strategies were mostly failures, and a parade of CEOs have come and gone as Burger King tries to find a winning idea to compete with the Golden Arches.

In America, Burger King is perceived to be the number two hamburger chain behind McDonald's, and it is in total sales. But the individual units lag far behind their "hamburger" competitors.

Wendy's, White Castle, Carl's Jr., Jack in the Box, Steak n Shake, and Whataburger all have higher per-unit sales.

In 2007, for example, Whataburger had 28 percent higher per-unit sales than Burger King.

The Bull fighter.

One of the most successful new product launches was the 1987 introduction of Red Bull. Today, the brand does $3.3 billion in worldwide sales.

One secret of Red Bull's success is its 8.3-ounce can. Like a stick of dynamite, a small can is a good visual hammer for an energy drink because it connotes the fact that the stuff is strong.

After Red Bull's rapid rise, almost every beverage company in the world tried to get into the energy-drink market.

Grocery and convenience stores were loaded with names like Red Stallion, RedLine, Red Devil, Red Alert, Pit Bull, Viva Toro, Blue Ox, Dark Dog, Power Horse USA, Bomba

Energy, Go-Go Energy, Hemp Soda, Deezel, Adrenaline Rush, Extreme Energy, Invigor8, Hype, Wired, and so on.

Naturally, they all came in 8.3-ounce cans.

Except Monster, one of the first energy drinks to come in a large sixteen-ounce can. Naturally, Monster rapidly became the second-largest-selling energy drink in America.

Instead of copying the Red Bull name and its 8.3-ounce can, Hansen Natural Corporation (Monster's owner) did just the opposite. What makes Monster's success so remarkable is the fact that its 16-ounce can is not a particularly good idea for an energy drink. An 8.3-ounce can does a much better job of connoting "energy."

In 2007, *Forbes* selected Hansen Natural as number one among the two hundred best small companies in America. Hansen's stock has increased eighty-four times in the five years since the end of 2002, the year Monster was introduced.

Where was Coca-Cola, the world's largest beverage company, when all this energy-drink action was taking place?

Copying the competition, of course. Coca-Cola's first try was KMX, an energy drink in the familiar 8.3-ounce can.

Next up was Full Throttle, an energy drink in a sixteen-ounce can, copying the Monster brand. Full Throttle is hanging in there, but is definitely not a monster brand.

Finally, Coca-Cola resorted to the big-company disease, line extension, and introduced Tab energy drink. Currently, Tab energy is an also-ran in a category with a lot of other also-rans.

The Champagne fighter.

Nobody has done a better marketing job than the producers of Champagne, the sparkling wine from the Champagne region of France. The Champagne name is so strong that most consumers think "sparkling wine" is an entirely different category.

Which creates a problem for Spain, one of the world's largest producers of sparkling wine. The Spanish product is called Cava, a word that connotes the caves where the sparkling wine is stored.

"Speaking of value," reported *Nation's Restaurant News,* "perhaps no country can compete with Spain for inexpensive sparkling wines."

And that's Cava's problem. It's imitation Champagne and it's "inexpensive."

Raise the price? Sales would drop like a rocket. Now it's imitation Champagne and expensive to boot.

On a number of occasions, we have tried to get the Cava producers to launch a "be-the-opposite" marketing program.

How can Cava be the opposite of Champagne?

Start with the bottles. Every Cava producer in Spain tries to hide the Cava name. On one leading brand, the Cava name is not even on the label. It's on the foil on top of the cork.

The name *Cava* should be as big and as bold as the brand name. (The Cava regulatory council, an industry body, should register Cava as a brand name in all the major countries of the world.)

What words come to mind when consumers think of Champagne?

"Special occasions."

Proof of this assumption is that global Champagne sales jumped 28.6 percent in the millennium year of 1999. The following year, Champagne sales promptly fell below their

1998 level. Even today, global Champagne sales have not topped 1999 levels.

Be the opposite. Cava should be for "everyday use." One way to express this concept: "Cava makes every day a special occasion."

(A typical restaurant experience: Order a $35 bottle of red or white wine and the waiter takes your order without comment. Order a $35 bottle of Cava and the waiter asks, "What are you celebrating?")

It's astounding how simple, conceptually sound concepts have the power to build dominant worldwide brands.

- "The ultimate driving machine."
- "A diamond is forever."
- "Cava makes every day a special occasion."

Why would Cava producers reject such an idea?

Because a slogan has no emotional power until it is endlessly repeated by consumers. "Just do it" had no emotional power until Nike launched a marketing program to exploit the idea.

It's difficult to recognize a good verbal idea. A constant refrain we have heard in the boardrooms of corporate America: "It doesn't turn me on."

As every marketing person knows, you don't get turned on by a new idea. You get turned on by your faith in marketing principles such as: "Be the opposite."

The caffe latte fighter.

Before Starbucks, there was Dunkin' Donuts, another coffee chain that had achieved a measure of success. It must be galling to the fifty-eight-year-old chain to see Starbucks preempt a product Dunkin' Donuts pioneered.

In the past few years, Dunkin' Donuts has been chasing the latest trends: bagels, muffins, hot sandwiches, and high-end coffee. All products in which it had no credibility.

Starbucks is not only a wake-up call but also an opportunity for Dunkin' Donuts. Its obvious approach is to go back to its coffee roots and then be the opposite.

Starbucks is expensive and slow and snobby. Good attributes for building a brand at the high end. But there are also opportunities at the low end.

Dunkin' Donuts is affordable, fast, and down-to-earth. A place without pretense, where hardworking Americans feel appreciated. To be truly successful, Dunkin' Donuts needs to focus on "fast."

Forget about "affordable." People already know that. Furthermore, affordable is not a benefit. It tells consumers that Dunkin' Donuts coffee is not as good as Starbucks coffee.

"Fast" has another benefit. It tells consumers their time is valuable. It has a special appeal to the upscale crowd headed for Starbucks.

Having to wait at Starbucks is the consumer's number one complaint, with cost right behind it.

Going after speed is going to require getting rid of some of the menu items at Dunkin'. And unless the company nails speed, it will never beat Starbucks. Consumers are willing to wait in a Starbucks, but not in a Dunkin' Donuts.

"It's Dunkin' Donuts Time." The place to stop for busy Americans who don't have the time (or the money) to waste at Starbucks.

What "Miller Time" did for beer (it took the brand from nowhere to number two, just behind Budweiser), "Dunkin' Donuts Time" could do for coffee.

You seldom see companies using simple marketing ideas like this because they almost never pass inspection by the left-brain management police.

It doesn't turn them on.

Hertz, Avis, Enterprise.

Founded in 1918, Hertz became America's leading car-rental company by being first in the category. And where did Hertz open its first establishment?

Keep in mind this was nine years before Charles Lindbergh's solo flight across the North Atlantic. When Hertz started, there were no airline passengers because there was no airline industry. Hertz opened where the customers were, in downtown locations. (Chicago was first.)

Founded in 1946, Avis did the opposite. Instead of competing head-to-head with Hertz, entrepreneur Warren Avis focused on airport locations and rapidly became the country's second-largest car-rental company.

Original name: Avis *Airlines* Rent-a-Car.

As airline traffic surged after the war, all the major car-rental companies shifted their operations to airline terminals, creating another opportunity to do the opposite.

Founded in 1957 as a car-leasing company by entrepreneur Jack Taylor, Enterprise Rent-A-Car started its rental business in the 1960s with locations in the suburbs. Its specialty: "insurance replacement."

Enterprise specialized in car rentals to consumers who needed a replacement car as the result of an accident, mechanical repair, or theft. Its marketing efforts were focused on referrals from insurance agents and adjusters. At one point, Enterprise CEO Andy Taylor, the founder's son, joked, "One of our biggest sales methods is doughnuts."

Enterprise dominates the car-rental business in the United States and is a larger company than Hertz. In a recent year, Enterprise had revenues of $9.0 billion and Hertz, $8.1 billion. Enterprise leads even though almost 90 percent of its locations are in the United States and Hertz operates in 145 countries around the world.

From downtown to airline terminals to the suburbs, at each stage of the car-rental game, conventional wisdom would have resisted the switch. It doesn't fit management thinking: "Go where the market is."

It does fit marketing thinking, however: "Go where the market isn't."

A strategy that can work in any category.

How did Lowe's, the number two chain, make substantial progress against Home Depot?

The leading home-improvement-warehouse chain, Home Depot is also a messy place originally designed that way to attract men.

So Lowe's made a special effort to be neat and clean, with wide aisles and brighter lighting—a place that was particularly attractive to women. In the process, Lowe's became the fastest-growing home-improvement chain.

Vlasic is the largest-selling pickle brand in America. So Claussen became a strong number two brand by moving from the shelf to the refrigerated section and calling itself the "crisp" pickle.

Montblanc marketed "fat" pens when its major competitor (Cross) was focused on selling "thin" pens.

Flip became the number one selling camcorder with 13 percent of the U.S. market in just a year. A tiny, stripped-down video recorder, Flip is the opposite of the big, complicated, expensive camcorders made by the large consumer electronics companies (Sony, Sanyo, Panasonic, Canon, JVC, and Samsung).

Callaway became the leading golf-club company by marketing oversize drivers (Big Bertha) when its major competitors were selling regular-size drivers.

Prince became the leading tennis-racket company by marketing oversize rackets when its major competitors were selling regular-size rackets.

Listerine is the bad-tasting mouthwash, so Scope became a strong number two brand by being the good-tasting mouthwash.

Barbie is a good-looking doll, so Bratz became a strong number two brand by being an ugly doll.

Traditional wedding and engagement rings were gold. So Scott Kay became one of the largest-selling jewelry brands in America by focusing on platinum. "The Platinum Generation."

And so it goes.

ValuJet's reputation suffered when it lost
one of its jets in the Florida Everglades.
Instead of spending millions to try to restore
its good name, the airline merged with AirTran.

CHAPTER 21

Management hates to change a name.
Marketing often welcomes a name change.

You might have missed the news, but Schlotzsky's, a 513-unit sandwich chain, filed for Chapter 11 bankruptcy.

What went wrong at Schlotzsky's? If you believe what you read in the paper, it was the usual things. Intense competition from other fast-food operators, a stale menu, poor operating procedures, not enough advertising.

When things go wrong, why does management never blame one of the most obvious factors? The name itself.

Schlotzsky's? Who can spell it? Who can pronounce it? Who can Google it? Furthermore, the first syllable in the name sounds dangerously close to *schlock,* Yiddish slang for cheap and shoddy.

"Most important marketing decision you can make."

Years ago, in a book called *Positioning,* we wrote, "In the positioning era, the single most important marketing decision you can make is what to name the product."

Today, twenty-seven years later, many left-brain management types are still not convinced. This is one reason why there are hordes of hopeless brand names in the market.

Not that some of these brands don't sell. Many do. If you price something cheap enough, it will move in spite of a dreadful name. Hyundai is selling almost half a million vehicles in America every year.

But did you ever hear someone say, "Eat your heart out; I just got myself a Hyundai"?

It gets worse. Hyundai's new Genesis model is designed to compete with Mercedes-Benz, BMW, and Lexus.

"We discussed quite a lot whether to launch a new brand or not," said one Hyundai executive, "but we decided to enhance the Hyundai brand image and make our dealers more profitable."

Instead of enhancing Hyundai's image, the Genesis is more likely to confuse it. "What? Forty-thousand for a Hyundai?"

Consumers find it exceedingly difficult to hang a positive perception on a negative name. (The name reminds us of a World War I battle cry: "Hun! Die!")

Management's arguments for not changing a name are always the same. It's not the name; it's the product, the service, the price.

That's not true at all. It's the perception of the product, the perception of the service, the perception of the price.

Along with a bad name comes a bad perception.

The Eastern problem.

We spent endless hours trying to convince a number of Eastern Air Lines executives that Eastern was a bad name for an airline. Especially for an airline that flew to the West Coast.

Even worse, "Eastern" is not synonymous with "good service." (Western may be, but not Eastern.)

The East, especially New York City, is synonymous with brash, rude, curt, insolent behavior. (Hey, it's a tough, fast-moving place with little time for the niceties of life.)

Former astronaut Frank Borman, Eastern's president at the time, disagreed. What you overlook, Mr. Borman wrote us, is the fact that "the name now has some forty-seven years behind it."

Common sense would have told you that you don't change a name that is forty-seven years old.

(Eastern Air Lines managed to live until age sixty before filing for bankruptcy protection.)

Even stranger is the saga of an Atlanta investment group that tried to raise $550 million to relaunch the airline as "New Eastern." Fortunately, the investment community wouldn't buy that piece of lunacy.

A bad name is a bad name. You can't change its perception by calling it "New Bad Name."

But there's a subtlety to marketing that management often misses.

Did we really want Eastern Air Lines to change its name? No, people would have thought that it was the old Eastern Air Lines with a new name.

Our recommendation? Merge with Western Airlines to create a legitimate reason for changing the airline's name. Furthermore, the combination of the two organizations would be perceived as a "national" airline, erasing Eastern's old "up-and-down the East Coast" reputation.

(At the time, Western Airlines was a viable merger candidate. It was eventually bought by Delta, an airline that didn't need a new name.)

"You can't change the name."

As marketing consultants, we are often approached by companies looking for a new strategy with one caveat: "You can't change the name."

Whoops. That rules us out for the assignment.

Canadian Airlines once approached us with the same caveat. But how could anyone possibly differentiate that airline from Air Canada, the dominant Canadian air carrier, without changing the name? It's impossible.

So did Cathay Pacific. Names are important. Consumers believe, rightly or wrongly, that the name a company uses has a real meaning. It's not just a name that happens to sail through a focus group without serious reservations.

We knew where the Pacific was. But where in the world is Cathay? You can't use Cathay on an airline, we told management, unless people know where it is. Another assignment we didn't get.

Pulte Homes, the nation's third-largest home builder, also approached us. We knew condo buyers were proud of their Trump apartments. But would home buyers be equally proud of their Pulte homes?

"I just bought a Pulte home." We couldn't visualize many home buyers bragging about their Pulte homes, so we told the company it needed a new name.

"Mr. Pulte would never agree" was the reply. That was another assignment we didn't get.

Where would Ralph Lifshitz be today if he had had the same attitude? Fortunately Mr. Lifshitz was astute enough to change his name to Ralph Lauren.

Consumers take names literally. I Can't Believe It's Not Butter is one of the best-selling margarines in America. "It must taste like butter," thinks the consumer, "otherwise they wouldn't have used that name."

Take Chi-Chi's, a casual-dining chain that went bankrupt a few years ago. What's a Chi-Chi, and who would possibly associate the name with the Mexican food it served? (With the strong trend toward Mexican food, it takes a particularly bad name to drive a Mexican chain out of business.)

How did a name like Chi-Chi's (Mexican slang for a woman's breasts) get selected in the first place? All too often, it's a question of fun and games in the boardroom. Come up with a cute name, do a little song and dance, get the crowd laughing, and you've made a sale.

Management, however, will shorten a name.

Surprisingly, there are times when management wholeheartedly agrees with a proposed name change. That's when someone wants to shorten the name or, even better, use initials instead of words.

Management is in love with initials and acronyms. They make extensive use of them in memos and e-mails. They memorize the stock symbols of companies they are interested in. (As TV viewers know quite well, you can't check stock prices on CNBC unless you know the initials used as stock symbols.)

Furthermore, if you want to sell everything under one brand name, as many management types do, then the name itself can't mean anything too specific. Initials fit this objective perfectly.

In our 1981 book, *Positioning*, we ranted and raved about what we called "the no-name trap." That year, there were twenty-seven "no-name" companies on *Fortune*'s list of the five hundred largest companies in America.

Today, there are forty-six. Tomorrow, there are likely to be more.

What drives a company to abandon a perfectly good name in favor of meaningless initials? There are two reasons.

One reason is the "shorter-is-better" argument. In today's fast-paced world, a long name is a handicap. So the advertising agency J. Walter Thompson changed its name to JWT.

J. Walter Thompson now goes into the history books, along with Doyle Dane Bernbach (changed to DDB) and Foote, Cone & Belding (changed to FCB.)

A second reason is a change in the marketplace. The J. Walter Thompson name is associated with traditional advertising, and the agency obviously wanted to broaden into non-traditional media like the Internet. They probably wanted a new name that wouldn't lock them into the past.

But the opposite happens. By using the initials JWT, the agency forever links its name to its J. Walter Thompson heritage.

It is almost impossible to create a separate perception for a set of initials than the perception created by the original words. Initials tend to remind people of the past.

Kentucky Fried Chicken wanted to distance itself from the unhealthy implications of the word "Fried." So they changed their name to KFC.

What happened next? When consumers see a KFC sign, they tend to think, "Kentucky Fried Chicken."

(KFC is having second thoughts about its initialization program. Some franchisees have been given the option of re-branding their stores as Kentucky Fried & Grilled Chicken.)

What do those initials stand for?

Consumers aren't dummies. When they see initials, they try to figure out what the initials stand for.

- GE conjures up General Electric.
- HP conjures up Hewlett-Packard.
- IBM conjures up International Business Machines.
- MTV conjures up Music Television.
- IRS conjures up Internal Revenue Service.
- FBI conjures up Federal Bureau of Investigation.
- USA conjures up United States of America.

Let's hope our new administration doesn't fall into the no-name trap, along the lines of: "We don't want to be considered as a conglomeration of individual states. We want to be considered as a single entity, a single country. Let's hire JWT, a division of WPP, to change our name to USA."

But what if a company's initials don't stand for anything to start with? Then the consumer is confused and is unlikely to remember the initials.

If you make your name famous, you can use your initials as a nickname. (Think JFK or FDR.) If your name isn't famous, using initials alone is almost certain to keep it from being famous.

Royal Philips Electronics selected NXP as the name of its newly independent semiconductor company. What does NXP stand for?

Nothing, but according to the company's chief executive, the name communicates "vibrancy and entertainment."

Wishful thinking, in our opinion. The NXP name communicates only one thing: What do those initials stand for?

Terms of endearment.

What complicates the name issue is trying to explain to management the role of a nickname.

Every brand needs two names: a real name and a nickname. Why is this? Because the use of nicknames help consumers establish closer relationships with brands they admire.

Notice, for example, when two people are exceptionally close, they almost never use their real names. It's always "sweetheart" or "honey" or "bunny" or some similar expression.

If your spouse legally changed his or her real name to "sweetheart" because that's the name you usually use, then guess what? You'd have to invent a new nickname.

JWT has just lost its nickname. What do we call the agency now?

J?

Should McDonald's change its name to Mickey D's because many consumers use those words as a nickname?

Not at all.

As a matter of fact, the Mickey D's name is one of the brand's best attributes. The name enhances McDonald's long-running advertising theme: "I'm loving it."

Should Harley-Davidson change its name to HOG, which is both its nickname and its new stock symbol?

(In a triple use of the nickname, HOG also stands for Harley Owners Group.)

Should Jennifer Lopez change her name to J. Lo?

Should Tom Cruise and Katie Holmes change their names to TomKat?

Should Brad Pitt and Angelina Jolie change their names to Brangelina?

Federal Express once had a great nickname, FedEx. Now that the company has changed its name to FedEx, what nickname can consumers use?

FE?

A wide variety of well-loved brands have nicknames that would be destroyed if those brands adopted their nicknames as their real names.

- American Express: AmEx
- Budweiser: Bud
- Coca-Cola: Coke
- Corvette : Vette
- *Cosmopolitan: Cosmo*
- Jaguar : Jag
- Macintosh: Mac
- Marks & Spencer: Marks & Sparks
- Stolichnaya: Stoli

What about management's "shorter-is-better" argument? It's true that consumers usually prefer a shorter brand name to a longer one.

Just look at the shelves in a supermarket that feature brands like All, Cheer, Crest, Dawn, Dial, Dove, Heinz, Lay's, Pam, Pert, Pledge, Post, Ritz, Scope, Silk, Tide, and a host of others.

Visually vs. verbally shorter.

The JWT name is visually shorter than the J. Walter Thompson name, but it's not verbally shorter.

Both are exactly the same length—five syllables. J-double-U-T. J-Wal-ter-Thomp-son.

Oddly, the verbal length of a brand name is more important than its visual length. That's because brands are built primarily by word of mouth. The shorter the verbal length, the easier it is for a consumer to pass along the name of the brand to friends, neighbors, and relatives.

As a matter of fact, consumers invariably try to shorten brand names to make this pass-along easier. Chevy instead of Chevrolet. Caddy instead of Cadillac. Mercedes instead of Mercedes-Benz.

In our experience, J. Walter Thompson was never known as JWT (five syllables.) It was always called J. Walter. (Three syllables.)

And Doyle Dane Bernbach was never DDB (three syllables.) It was always Doyle Dane (two syllables.)

Likewise Foote, Cone & Belding was never FCB (three syllables.) It was always Foote Cone (two syllables.)

Almost always, consumers pick nicknames that are verbally shorter than the real brand names. Occasionally, they will use a nickname that is the same verbal length as the brand name (Mickey D's example.) But seldom will they use nicknames that are verbally longer.

Would someone please explain to us why the management at Northwest (two syllables) paints its planes with a NWA logotype? Does anyone use NWA (five syllables) as a nickname for Northwest Airlines? We think not.

Fortunately, the merger with Delta solves that problem.

Words are more potent than initials.

The best proof is the widespread use of words rather than initials. Whenever possible, consumers will try to convert a set of initials into an acronym.

- "Radar" instead of R-D-A-R for "radio detecting and ranging."
- "Laser" instead of L-A-S-E-R for "light amplification by stimulated emission of radiation."
- "Gap" instead of G-A-A-P for "generally accepted accounting principles."

When given a choice, most everyone prefers words. You could use A-I-D-S for "acquired immunodeficiency syndrome," but almost nobody does. Most people just say "aids."

Why is this? The word "aids" is shorter (one syllable) than the initials (four syllables.)

Across the street from a YMCA in Atlanta is an IHOP restaurant. Why do people say "Y-M-C-A" (four syllables) and not "I-H-O-P" (also four syllables)?

Because they found a way to convert IHOP into a two-syllable acronym: "I-hop."

Notwithstanding these arguments, management continues to initialize corporate America. In February 2006, the $3.9 billion Computer Associates International officially changed its name to CA, Inc.

CA is a nice nickname, but, unfortunately, the U.S. Postal Service has already awarded it to the state of California.

Computers.

Software.

Consumer electronics.

Cellphones.

Thanks to constant product innovation,
Apple has a foot in four different markets.
Someday the innovations will dry up
and the company's troubles will start.

CHAPTER 22

Management is bent on constant innovation. Marketing is happy with just one.

Sharper Image, home of innovative products such as the Razor scooter, the robotic dog, the Ionic Breeze, the StressEraser, and the R2-D2 interactive droid, has filed for Chapter 11 bankruptcy.

Innovation is not a marketing strategy, and companies that count on a constant flow of new, innovative products will someday find themselves in deep trouble. As Sharper Image did.

Every successful company needs a marketing strategy that may or may not include innovation. Yet many management gurus have elevated "innovation" to a point where it is widely perceived as the single most important function of a corporation.

Witness the raft of recent books and articles on innovation. There's also the famous Peter Drucker quote: "The business enterprise has two—and only these two—basic functions: marketing and innovation."

Innovation is optional.

A business enterprise has one basic function, in our opinion: "Build a brand that can dominate a category."

Early on, innovation can help a company build that kind of brand.

- Instant photography and Polaroid
- The minicomputer and Digital Equipment
- The plain-paper copier and Xerox
- The microprocessor and Intel
- Wireless e-mail and BlackBerry
- The athletic shoe and Nike

But when a category matures, the situation changes. Take the automotive industry. The significant innovations in the auto industry took place decades ago: the V-8 engine, automatic transmission, power steering, air-conditioning, seat belts, air bags, and so on.

What makes an effective automobile brand today is not innovation but rather a narrow focus on an attribute or a segment of the market. Reliability and Toyota. Driving and BMW. Youth and Scion.

Innovations outside of a brand's core position can undermine a brand. What did the PT Cruiser do for Chrysler, except to confuse customers? What did the Phaeton do for Volkswagen? The Viper for Dodge?

Dodge is a big-truck brand. Does the truck buyer prefer Dodge because it accelerates like a Viper?

Marketing people know that most brands don't need innovations. They need to figure out what they stand for (or what they could stand for) and then how to use marketing tactics to "own" that concept in consumers' minds.

An innovation like New Coke almost killed the brand.

Sacrifice builds brands.

Not innovation. Search was a commodity on the Internet until the arrival of Google.

Google narrowed its focus to search only and in the process build a mighty brand. So what is Google doing lately?

They're innovating. The company is even spending hundreds of millions of dollars to innovate in alternative energy sources such as solar, geothermal, and wind power.

The March 2008 issue of *Fast Company* features "the world's 50 most innovative companies." As you might expect, number one is Google.

The magazine devotes eighteen pages to the Google story. Prospective employees are often asked, "If you could change the world using Google's resources, what would you build?"

Our answer would have been "We'd use the resources to build a second brand, like Toyota did with Lexus, instead of using the resources to sabotage the base brand."

Then there's Apple, which seems to be an exception. Certainly Apple has been successful because of the widely held belief that all its products are highly innovative.

That's true today, but what about tomorrow? Innovation cannot last forever. Sooner or later, Apple is going to run up against a brick wall and find itself fighting a host of competitors that dominate its categories.

Apple doesn't dominate any category except MP3 players, yet manages to compete successfully against Hewlett-Packard and Dell in personal computers. Against Nokia and Motorola in cell phones. Against Sony and Samsung in consumer electronics. Against Microsoft in personal-computer operating systems. That's a situation that cannot last. As the categories mature, Apple is bound to run out of innovative new ideas.

Then there's Enron, which *Fortune* named "America's most-innovative company" for five years in a row from 1996 to 2000. The following year, the company went bankrupt.

A gas-pipeline company, Enron "innovated" itself into a host of online businesses, including the buying and selling of oil, natural gas, electricity, high-speed data transmission, newsprint, television advertising, and so on.

Fraud didn't get Enron into trouble. Trouble got Enron into fraud.

Executives at profitable companies don't generally cook the books. The huge losses sustained by Enron's foolish strategy pushed the company's management over the edge.

Innovation can destroy a brand's authenticity.

Take Jack Daniel's, the largest-selling bourbon and the fifth-largest-selling liquor in the world. The label looks like it hasn't changed since the distillery was opened in 1866 (the first in the United States). "Jack Daniel's Old Time Old No. 7 Brand" is what the label says.

In case the message didn't register, the label also says, "Whiskey made as our fathers made it for 7 generations."

In liquor, in wine, in beer, in soft drinks, in food, in tools, and in many other categories, right-brain marketers try to keep a consistent look and a consistent message. That's what communicates the authenticity of the brand.

Often, a newly arrived CEO wants to use innovation

to put his or her stamp on the brand. The temptations are sometimes too much to resist.

No category has seen as many innovations as cola. Over the years, Pepsi-Cola has introduced Diet Pepsi, Pepsi One, Pepsi A.M., Pepsi Kona, Pepsi Light, Pepsi Edge, Pepsi Max, Pepsi XL, Pepsi-Cola Retro, Pepsi Blue, Diet Pepsi Jazz, Pepsi Raw, and Pepsi N.F.L. Kickoff.

(This list doesn't include the many flavor variations Pepsi has introduced, including vanilla, cherry, lime, etc.)

Typical quote: "Pepsi Blue has the potential to reinvigorate the cola category," said a company executive. "We're convinced innovation is the key to growth."

In the United Kingdom, the company is launching Pepsi Raw, the healthy cola, which a top executive called "the most significant innovation from Pepsi U.K. in the last 15 years."

Over at Coca-Cola, the innovations also roll out on a regular basis. The latest is Diet Coke Plus, with five essential vitamins and minerals.

Meanwhile, per capita consumption of cola in the United States continues its slow decline as consumers switch to water and other healthier beverages.

A company should spend its innovation money to create new brands, not to salvage existing brands. Why didn't Coke put the five essential vitamins and minerals into water instead of cola? The company could have saved the $4.1 billion it spent to buy Vitaminwater-maker Glacéau.

As the Sharper Image story demonstrates, innovation is not a strategy. It's a tactic that needs to be used in support of a company's marketing strategy.

The one machine that mixes slides, movies and sound.

Now you can put all of the zap, and creative bam of a full-fledged multi-media presentation on your prospect's desk. Or place it at the point of sale. In one machine. The Norelco PIP® projector.

Single frame to full motion.

Norelco created a super 8 projector with variable speed, so you could use slides where you want razor sharp still frames, and movies where you want action. Or anything in between.

The nice thing about our approach is that it gives promotion-minded people a new kind of medium. Not merely by combining the techniques of motion, slide, and overhead projection into one machine, but by putting the full impact of its presentation against content rather than execution. It's multi media where the medium doesn't have to be the message.

The creative machine.

The Norelco multi-media projection system allows the creative-minded person to swing freely. There are no limitations we can think of to frustrate even the most unique idea. On the contrary, Norelco makes it easy to use such things as stop-action, freeze frames, slow downs, speed-ups, build-ups, even frame changing to a musical beat.

Putting all of these effects together into a multi-media presentation can be relatively simple. A number of companies have actually produced their own programs, often using existing materials for a large portion of their presentation.

The versatile machine.

The Norelco multi-media projector operates on a simple "dual cassette" system. A tape cassette that contains the sound and advance pulses. And a super 8mm cassette for the visuals.

Since audio and visual cassettes are separate, you can use this machine in interesting ways. Any number of audio cassettes can be made for the same visual cassette. So you can convert a "his" presentation to a "hers." A salesman's training version to a prospect's selling version. And you can translate into the language of any of your markets.

From autos to hypodermics.

The adaptability of our projector to sales and training objectives has been proved in a wide range of industries. One of Detroit's big three for service training. A clothing manufacturer for public relations. A pharmaceutical company for product demonstration.

A top flight manufacturer of private planes has taken advantage of just about everyone of its features in a precedent-setting 30-hour course on the fundamentals of flight as well as basic instructions in flying.

Before your next presentation gets into or out of the storyboard stage, you ought to take a close look at the Norelco projector. First, because it can add the drama and impact of a movie at little more than the cost of a slide presentation. Second, because it is incredibly easy for anyone to use. In fact it is almost foolproof. There's nothing to thread or anything else to fumble. You know how easy it is to snap in a cassette.

Move up to multi media.

Let us demonstrate the multi-media projector that interests you most; rear-screen or wall projection models, with or without viewer-response capability. To set up a date call Bob Higgins at 201-267-3802.

For catalog and prices write, North American Philips Corp., Training & Education Systems Division, 35 Abbett Avenue, Morristown, N.J. 07960. *Norelco*

The multi-media projector by Norelco.

Almost thirty years ago, Norelco introduced
the nation's first multimedia projector
to handle slides, movies, and sound.
The multimedia product went nowhere.

CHAPTER 23

Management has the hots for multimedia. Marketing is not so sure.

Playboy is digitizing its entire archive. All 636 issues of the magazine will be rendered page by page on six disks, one for each decade. Price: $100 per disk.

What a mistake.

Every time a new medium arrives, management thinks, "What an opportunity to extend our franchise." So magazines and newspapers and radio and TV outlets are jumping all over themselves to digitize their brands.

What left-brain management sees as an opportunity, right-brain marketing sees as a loss of focus.

The Bunny's sorry history.

Over the years, *Playboy* has extended its brand into clubs, casinos, books, videos, cable channels, calendars, clothing, condoms, cigars, and cola, among other things.

In 1971, Playboy went public for $23.50 a share.

Current price: $1.92 a share.

In the past ten years, Playboy Enterprises had revenues of $3.2 billion, yet managed to lose $90.3 million.

In spite of these dismal results, many experts applaud the Playboy approach. Here's how a founding partner of a worldwide management consulting company, and the author of six books on strategic thinking, describes the Playboy approach:

"A user/customer class–driven company is one that has deliberately anchored its entire business around a describable and specific category of end users or customers. The company then tries to satisfy a range of related needs that stem from that class of end user . . . Playboy, for instance, is a good example of a company pursuing a user class-driven strategy. The phrase 'entertainment for men' on its magazine cover spells it out quite clearly."

Does this all make sense? Sure, it does. But common sense is not marketing sense.

Playboy fell into the line-extension trap, the most common management mistake. Digitizing its magazine is only the latest in a long line of similar mistakes.

A guy who lives in his pajamas in a Holmby Hills mansion might not get the respect of the media mavens, but the truth is, much of the media industry is making the same mistake as Playboy.

All Talk and no action.

Line extension used to be a disease of consumer-goods companies only. But the disease has been spreading.

Take *Talk* magazine, or rather Talk Media, a company founded in 1998 by Tina Brown and financed by Miramax, a division of Disney.

The former editor of *Vanity Fair* and *The New Yorker,* Ms. Brown announced that she would, according to the *New York Times,* "publish a new monthly magazine, publish books and produce films and television programming."

Twenty-nine months after its launch, *Talk* magazine folded, losing a reported $54 million, including the money spent on a launch party on Liberty Island for fourteen hundred of the world's most famous people.

Multimedia has been a buzzword for years. "Investors just can't get enough of multimedia," reported *BusinessWeek.* "Wall Street has bid up the shares of almost all media companies, figuring they'll offer much of the information that will give multimedia zing. Most publishers, meanwhile, are rushing to set up on-line services."

When was this published? Last week? Last month? Last year?

No. *BusinessWeek* reported on the multimedia movement in its December 6, 1993, issue. That's more than fifteen years ago.

The most dangerous words in the dictionary.

Multimedia, multiplatform, multifunction, multichannel, multidigital, multifaceted. Whenever you hear a word starting with "multi," you can be pretty sure it's a sign of trouble.

Did Harvey Weinstein, founder of Miramax Films with his brother Bob, learn anything from the Talk Media disaster. We're afraid not.

His new venture is making the same mistake. "The Weinstein Co. is positioned more as a diversified boutique media company," says *Time* magazine, "encompassing home video, cable television, Broadway theater, book publishing, video games and, of course, the Internet."

"We've already done a movie company," said Harvey Weinstein. "Today we're in the business of providing content and our own distribution pipelines."

Early returns are not good. According to a Weinstein board member quoted in *Fortune,* "This fiscal year has been a disappointing one."

Media moguls mainly think in "multi" terms. Michael Eisner, former CEO of Walt Disney, put together some $385 million to acquire Topps, the maker of Bazooka bubble gum and baseball cards.

"Topps is a brand that's in the brain-waves of about 70 years of the American male," said Mr. Eisner. "I can take that affinity and turn it into a sports-media company."

Turning bubble gum into a media empire doesn't seem to be much of a problem for a media mogul. "Mostly, it's making Topps—through the media of filmed entertainment, internet and television, through the cards and taking them to the digital world—to turn it into a far bigger media company than it is today," said Mr. Eisner.

The bubble-gum bubble is about to burst, in our opinion.

Then there's Steve Case, the brains behind America Online. After his disastrous merger with Time Warner, Mr. Case his turned his talents in another direction. His new company: Revolution LLC.

What market is Revolution trying to revolutionize? Actually there are four markets.

- Revolution Health, with retail clinics and Web sites
- Revolution Money, a PIN-based credit-card and payment platform

- Revolution Places, offering luxury-resort experiences
- Revolution Living, with controlling interests in a spa and a car-sharing service

Business is often compared to warfare. And one of the classic stories from World War II is the failure of Operation Market Garden. Or, as it is known in military history, *A Bridge Too Far*.

Revolution LLC is three bridges too far.

All content is not alike.

Management and marketing tend to think on different levels. (Naturally management is on the top level.)

For example, the ten of diamonds, playing cards, and games are three different levels of abstraction. Marketing thinks in terms of the "ten of diamonds." Management thinks in terms of "games."

To a marketing person, an article in the *New York Times* is a lot different than a Hollywood movie. But not to a management mogul.

To a management mogul, "content is content." The only difference is how it's packaged and where it's viewed.

According to CEO Mark Hurd, here's where Hewlett-Packard is headed: "To integrate content across the home, whether it's emanating from the web, from satellites, from cable, or the PC, and bring that to the consumer's touch."

Sir Howard Stringer, CEO of Sony, said something similar: "Synergy is back with a vengeance and I don't have to defend myself anymore because the ability to access content any time, anywhere on any kind of device is now accepted."

There's an assumption that the sender provides the content and the receiver decides the medium in which he or she wants to read, listen, or view the content. If only life were simple.

Why in the world would anyone claim that television is dead and that everybody is going to watch video on their computers or (even worse) on their cell phones?

Yet that's what Bill Gates predicted at a recent *Wall Street Journal* conference.

(Television is still alive and well. More people are watching more television on their TV sets than they ever did. According to Nielsen, the average American spent 127 hours with TV in May 2008 compared with 121 hours in May 2007. The comparable number for the Internet was 26 hours, up from 24 hours in 2007.)

New brands vs. line-extended brands.

The most successful Internet brands have been new brands like Google, Yahoo!, Amazon, eBay, YouTube, MySpace, Facebook, Priceline.com, craigslist, Wikipedia, AOL, and so on.

Every print publication thinks it needs to expand into the Internet to be successful. It's exactly the opposite. Stay where you are and launch a new brand on the Net.

There are, of course, some small multimedia successes. Perhaps the most notable of the multiplatform operators is the *Wall Street Journal,* with some 931,000 subscribers to its online service.

But we question whether the *Journal* is a "financial" multimedia success. In spite of the fact that the *Journal* is one of the most respected publications in the country, it reportedly lost money in 2007.

It was back in 1996 that the *Wall Street Journal* launched its

Interactive Edition, which later became the *Wall Street Journal Online*. That was two years before Google was founded.

Today, Google is worth $91.6 billion on the stock market, while Dow Jones was bought by Rupert Murdoch's News Corporation for $5.7 billion.

Instead of launching an online edition of the *Wall Street Journal*, what if the management people at Dow Jones had said to themselves, "What can we do on the Internet that takes advantage of the unique properties of the new medium?

"What's the biggest problem faced by newspaper reporters and editors?

"It's finding authoritative sources for facts and figures that help dramatize and illuminate newspaper stories. What if we launched an Internet search site that would help our people instantly dig out those facts and figures?"

What if the *Wall Street Journal* had launched a "Google" instead of an online edition of the newspaper? Maybe Dow Jones would still be an independent company.

A buzzword is a pit bull.

Yet the multimedia craze will probably be with us for a long time. Once a buzzword grips the imagination of an industry, it seldom lets go.

You might think Lifetime is just a cable TV network. Wrong.

"Lifetime has the opportunity, if we play it right," said CEO Betty Cohen, "to be the leading integrated electronic media company for women. That's what we should be. Not just a cable network."

You might think the American Business Press is just an organization of trade-paper publishers. Wrong.

The American Business Press is now the American Business Media.

You might think Condé Nast just publishes magazines. Wrong.

"Condé Nast does not like being called a mere magazine company, although it publishes 27," reported the *New York Times*. "We're content providers," said Richard D. Beckman, president of the Condé Nast media group.

You might think *USA Today* is just a newspaper. Wrong.

According to publisher and president Tom Curley, "We are no longer a newspaper; we are a network. We feed content to television. We feed content to the Internet from the same core platform." *Advertising Age* called *USA Today* "a multi-platform media brand."

You might think ESPN is just a television company. Wrong.

"We are not a television company," says ESPN executive John Skipper. "We're gonna surround consumers with media."

Even product companies are getting into the act. You might think that Lionel is a just a model-train maker. Wrong.

According to the *Wall Street Journal*, Lionel's chief executive sees the firm as "an entertainment company and not just a toy maker."

You might think a recent conference sponsored by the Television Bureau of Advertising would focus solely on TV. Wrong.

For the first time, the conference was developed to a single topic: the importance of the multiplatform. That is, offering content and advertising not only on local broadcast stations but also online, on cell phones and other wireless devices, through video on demand, and on video iPods.

You might think *TV Guide* is just a magazine. Wrong.

"With proven multiplatform success for dozens of advertisers, *TV Guide* understands the needs of today's marketers and can deliver strategic programs for any category." These include magazine, channel, interactive program guides, on demand-video, online and mobile.

You might think Time Inc. is just a magazine publisher. Wrong.

"I've got a thousand brilliant print-sales people who are going to be transformed into a thousand brilliant multimedia salespeople," said Ann Moore, chairman and chief executive of Time Inc. "We are a content company, OK? We create and we edit, and we aggregate the best content out there. We can deliver to you, our reader, in whatever format you want it in the future——maybe not on paper."

One of this book's coauthors used to be a big believer in multimedia. Years ago, his agency was hired by Norelco to advertise the company's new multimedia projector and he got very excited about the product.

Needless to say, the multimedia projector went nowhere.

The 150 empty calories in a can of Coke
was bound to hurt the brand in the long term.
Tab could have been its brand of the future.
Instead the company focused on Diet Coke.

CHAPTER 24

Management focuses on the short term. Marketing focuses on the long term.

Harold Geneen, the quintessential conglomerator, had a favorite expression: "If you make your quarters, you'll make your year."

Another favorite expression of the former CEO of ITT: "There will be no long-range planning."

The conglomerates of yesterday are mostly gone, but that kind of management thinking still lingers on. "Make your quarters and things will work out."

A short-term hit for a long-term future.

Marketing has a different approach. There comes a time when a company has to shift gears.

PepsiCo took a gigantic short-term hit in 1997 when it spun off its restaurant chains (Pizza Hut, Kentucky Fried Chicken, and Taco Bell) to focus on its beverage business, a strategy recommended before the fact in our 1996 book *Focus: The Future of Your Company Depends on It.*

There were sound marketing reasons for making the

move. PepsiCo was getting hammered by Coca-Cola on the fountain side of its business. Headline of a typical Coke advertisement: "Has PepsiCo opened a restaurant near you yet? Wait four hours."

The ad continued, "Because every four hours PepsiCo adds another unit to their restaurant empire. Another unit that competes with your business and feeds your customers."

In contrast, Coca-Cola promised "commitment," not "competition"—pretty strong stuff, and pretty effective in maintaining Coca-Cola's massive share of the fountain business.

The restaurant-chain spin-off cleared the decks for Pepsi-Co's 2000 acquisition of Quaker Oats and its Gatorade brand, an addition that greatly strengthened PepsiCo's beverage lineup.

"One step backward, two steps forward" is the general principle.

In our strategy work, we often recommend that a company discontinue extraneous products and services (that's the one step backward) and then find a focus that will drive the company's business in the future (that's the two steps forward.)

Years ago, we tried this approach with a famous software company. "What? You want to jeopardize a $75 million a year revenue stream?" was the CEO's response. (The famous software company is no longer in business.)

"If you keep on doing what you always did," goes the old motto, "you'll keep on getting what you always got." The way to break that pattern is to shift gears and make changes.

That's the one step backward that managers who manage "by the quarters" will seldom make.

Bumping up against the ceiling.

Companies often find that, except for the effects of inflation, growth is hard to come by. And so the emphasis shifts
to cutting costs and firing people.

Coca-Cola is one of those companies. During the sixteen-
year reign of Roberto Goizueta (from 1981 to his death in
1997), Coca-Cola's stock-market value increased from $4.0
billion to $145.0 billion. In the eleven years since, Coke's
stock market value has gone sideways. The last time we
checked, it was $101.4 billion.

What went wrong at Coca-Cola?

Nothing.

It's a classic case of cause and effect. The cola market went
sideways (cause), so the stock went sideways (effect.)

At least the Coca-Cola Company didn't lose its focus by
buying restaurant chains. Instead, Coke kept its focus on the
beverage business. Good marketing thinking.

What's not good marketing thinking is how the company
handled its crown jewel, the Coca-Cola brand.

One reason kids are turning away from Coke and Pepsi is the
150 calories in each can. Slim is in and fat is out, although the
concept is more observed in theory than in practice.

With all the publicity about the dangers of obesity, you
might think that Diet Coke and Diet Pepsi would greatly
outsell their full-calorie siblings, but they don't. The last
time we checked, the diet flavors of Coca-Cola represented
only 41 percent of the brand's sales volume.

What should Coca-Cola have done?

Launch a separate cola brand with zero calories that ap-
pealed to the younger generation.

Actually, they did. The brand was called Tab, and it used to be the market leader in diet colas. (The day Diet Coke was launched, Tab was the No.1 diet cola, ahead of Diet Pepsi by 32 percent.)

What killed Tab was a tactical mistake, although it was done deliberately. The company kept the latest sweetener (aspartame) out of Tab and reserved it for Diet Coke. Tab was stuck with saccharin.

Today, younger people perceive Diet Coke as a brand for older people on a diet. And men perceive Diet Coke to be a brand for women. Not exactly the perceptions that are going to make Diet Coke the hip beverage of the twenty-first century.

Tab versus Diet Coke is a good example of long-term versus short-term thinking. In the short term, Diet Coke was hugely successful. A year after its launch, the product became the best-selling low-calorie soft drink. Ultimately, it was voted the best new product of the decade of the 1980s.

But in the long term, Tab would have been the better choice. Instead of being perceived as an inferior version of Coca-Cola (Diet Coke's perception), Tab could have been positioned as a totally separate product. In essence, the cola brand of the future.

Recently, Coca-Cola tried another line extension designed to reach the younger crowd. It's called Coke Zero, a brand that has been a moderate success.

Zero is a nice name, but the Coke half of the name locks the brand into the past. Furthermore, the company is undermining its Zero name by using it also on Sprite and Powerade.

Too bad. One of the reasons for cola's outstanding success is its multiple flavor "notes." Ginger ale tastes like ginger. Lemonade tastes like a lemon. An orange drink tastes like an orange.

But a cola drink combines many flavors: caramelized sugar, vanilla, orange, lemon, lime, and a number of spices.

Like fine wines, which also feature multiple flavors, colas are not a boring drink. A cola drinker seldom tires of the taste. Cola could still have a bright future, but not if it gets labeled as unfashionable. And not without the launch of a second brand by one of the major cola companies.

One of the most difficult problems in marketing is balancing the needs of today with the future needs of tomorrow. While Diet Coke was obviously successful in the short term, its long-term success is in doubt.

Furthermore, Diet Coke is a brand whose obvious target is regular Coca-Cola. It has been positioned as "The taste of Coke without the calories."

It's a branding teeter-totter. When one goes up, the other goes down.

Microsoft goes soft.

Another company bumping up against the ceiling is Microsoft. In fiscal 2002, Microsoft stock hit $35.00 a share. In the five years since, it never reached that level again. The last time we checked, the stock was at $20.30.

When things go soft, management has two choices: fix the problem, or hide the problem by buying somebody. Microsoft tried to buy Yahoo! for $44.6 billion. (From a marketing point of view, this was not a good idea because it would cause the company to lose its focus.)

What is Microsoft's problem? Its Windows operating system, its crown jewel. Windows Vista, the latest version of the Windows operating system, has taken six years and $6 billion to develop.

What happened to Windows is exactly what happened to Coca-Cola.

- When nutritionists questioned the 150 calories in a can, Coca-Cola added diet versions.
- When parents questioned the 45 milligrams of caffeine in a can, Coca-Cola added decaffeinated versions.
- When consumers started to switch to fruit drinks, Coca-Cola added cherry, lemon, and lime versions.
- When consumers started to switch to vitamin-enhanced water, Coca-Cola added a vitamin version (Coke Plus).

Coca-Cola wound up with fourteen different flavors. So far, Microsoft has introduced only six flavors of Windows, which is probably five too many.

The six flavors are: Windows Starter 2007, Windows Vista Enterprise, Windows Vista Home Basic, Windows Vista Home Premium, Windows Vista Ultimate, and Windows Vista Business.

Vista is too big, too bloated with features, too complicated, and too expensive. Its future is in doubt.

One brand for today. One brand for tomorrow.

As far as brands are concerned, left-brain management people are single-minded: "Put everything into our core brand, no matter how many line extensions it takes." That might work in the short term, but not in the long term.

Right-brain marketing people think differently. As a discipline, marketing is basically a long-term proposition in which a new strategy can take years to bear fruit.

Marketing people are much more likely to say, "Keep the core brand focused and deal with tomorrow by launching a second brand. Or even a third or a fourth brand."

Why should the screen of a personal computer look like the instrument panel of a Boeing 747?

Microsoft should launch a second operating-system brand that dramatically reduces complexity for the vast majority of consumers who use a computer for its basic functions: e-mail, Web surfing, and photo filing.

Of course, such a system would mean starting from scratch, with little or no compatibility with existing software. That's the one step backward.

Then let the marketing folks take over. Simplicity is not the way to position the new brand. "Hey, stupid, have we got the software for you."

Speed is the new position. Computers are blindingly fast. Current software, hobbled by Windows, is agonizingly slow. Lee Gomes, writing in the *New York Times,* reports that readers of his column keep asking, "Why is it that every new version of Windows requires more memory and a faster CPU, yet runs slower than the last one?"

Any ordinary personal computer can alphabetize a random list of a thousand words or so in half a second. Yet to start up that same computer from scratch might take two or three minutes.

How many people would buy a cell phone that takes two or three minutes to establish a connection?

How many people would buy an automobile that moans

and groans in the garage for two or three minutes before you can drive it out?

An automobile that can go from zero to one hundred miles per hour in half a second won't sell if it takes three minutes to back it out of the garage.

A blindingly fast operating system could be Microsoft's brand of the future. That's the two steps forward.

We can visualize Microsoft's reaction: "What? You want to jeopardize a $17-billion-a-year revenue stream?"

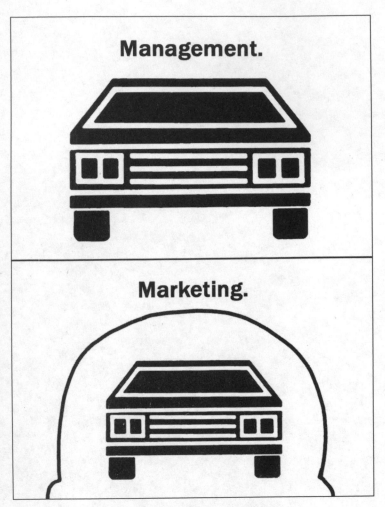

Management believes the key to success is
developing a better product.
Marketing believes the key to success is
developing a better perception.

CHAPTER 25

Management counts on common sense. Marketing counts on marketing sense.

Common sense is the gulf between logical, analytical, left-brain management types and intuitive, holistic, right-brain marketing types.

The more experience a marketing person has, the more he or she realizes that common sense is usually wrong.

"Marketing takes a day to learn," says Phil Kotler, America's most famous marketing professor, "but a lifetime to master."

How do marketing people deal with chief executive officers who have the power to make strategic marketing decisions without the experience only a lifetime of marketing can accumulate?

We wish we knew.

Many losing battles.

We have spent many days in many boardrooms in many countries arguing with CEOs and their staffs.

"Nice presentation, but we'll do it my way," says the typical CEO, "and I'm counting on our marketing team to do a great job executing our new strategy."

Marketing is 90 percent strategy and 10 percent execution. With the right product, the right name, the right target audience, the right position, and the right timing, most marketing programs are bound to work. The difficult part is the 90 percent. The easy part is the 10 percent.

Execution depends primarily on people. And people are people. If two companies each employ some one thousand people, it's almost impossible for one company to have more than a tiny edge over the other in terms of the capabilities of its people.

Furthermore, good strategy improves execution. As a matter of fact, good strategy can be defined as a strategy that will allow better, more-consistent execution.

"We fall into error," says history's greatest military strategist, Carl von Clausewitz, "if we attribute to strategy a power independent of tactical results."

Most management publications are also focused on execution. *Fortune* once reported, "Ninety percent of organizations fail to execute on otherwise well-planned strategies."

But if they failed to execute the strategies, how does one determine they were "well-planned" in the first place?

Good execution cannot change or improve a poor marketing strategy.

On the side of common sense are the management people, who approach every situation in a sane, sensible way. Their emphasis is always on the product: "If we can produce a better product at a better price, we can win the battle."

What frustrates marketing people is the fact that management's emphasis on common sense rules out the possibility there might be an illogical, uncommonsense "marketing idea" that can drive a company's business.

Ideas don't matter?

"Management, I had discovered, is not something mysterious or conceptually difficult," writes Charles Handy, a global-management guru and founder of the London Business School. "Its difficulty lies in applying the ideas, not in the ideas themselves."

Sure, management is not conceptually difficult if you believe there aren't any worthwhile conceptual ideas out there.

Marketing ideas are conceptually difficult because they contradict common sense. Because they deal with changing human perceptions, an enormously difficult task. Ask any psychiatrist or psychologist.

Guess who is winning the battle of the boardroom?

It's not the uncommonsense or marketing side. It's the management side.

When a company gets into trouble, the solutions are always the same commonsense solutions: Improve the products. Cut the costs. Reduce the prices.

Then hold employee meetings and talk about loyalty, enthusiasm, and team building.

Line extension rules the roost.

Take line extension, which has become an article of faith in the management community. We have fought repeatedly with management people on this single issue.

Guess what name Western Union decided to use when the company went into the telephone business? It was a common-sense decision.

Western Union was a well-known company with more than a hundred years of history. Why couldn't they use their old, famous Western Union name on their new telephone business?

It was the "commonsense" decision, of course, but one that eventually caused the company a $600 million write-off.

Guess what name Kodak decided to use when the company went into the copier business in competition with Xerox, Canon, and Ricoh?

The Kodak name, of course. Another "commonsense" decision that turned into a marketing disaster.

Guess what name Xerox decided to use when the company went into the mainframe computer business?

The Xerox name, of course. After spending almost a billion dollars to buy Scientific Data Systems, Xerox figured its own name was a lot better known. True, but the perception was wrong.

Guess what name IBM decided to use when the company went into the personal-computer business? And guess who won the PC battle?

A battle that took place between the world's most powerful company at the time (IBM) and a sophomore at the University of Texas (Michael Dell.)

Common sense would have told you that Dell didn't have a chance competing with IBM in personal computers.

Guess what name Barnes & Noble decided to use when the company launched an Internet book site to compete with Amazon.com? And guess who won that battle?

It wasn't BarnesandNoble.com. It was the Internet site launched by thirty-one-year-old Jeff Bezos, a man who had no prior experience selling books.

Booz & Company.

Guess what name Booz Allen Hamilton decided to use when they spun off their global, commercial management consulting practice into a separate company?

That's right. Booz & Company.

That's typical management thinking. Names don't matter—and even if they do, the new company can take advantage of the reputation of the ninety-four-year-old Booz Allen Hamilton.

In a moment of madness, the management consultants have created two long-term marketing problems for themselves.

One problem is the Booz name. Will employees be known as "Boozers"? Let's hope not.

The second problem is the confusion between the two companies: Booz Allen Hamilton, a management consulting company specializing in U.S. government work, and Booz, a global commercial management consulting company.

Names don't matter to left-brain management types. But they do matter to consumers and to right-brain marketing types, who spend their entire careers studying consumer behavior including the effects of names, good and bad.

Lawyers, accountants, and marketing people.

Also lining up with management people on the common-sense side of the table are the lawyers and the accountants. They get along quite well.

When management has a legal problem, it turns to its lawyers and invariably takes their advice.

When management has an accounting problem, it turns to its CPAs and invariably takes their advice.

When management has a marketing problem, it turns to its marketing people and says, "We'll do it my way because marketing is just common sense. And no one has more common sense than the CEO, right?"

Right.

But common sense doesn't work in business today. The only thing that works in business today is marketing sense.

The battle isn't over.

As a matter of fact, the war has just begun. Every year, a new generation of MBAs arrives on the scene, ready to take their place on management's side of the table.

Every year, management dogma is reinforced by some of the most important newspapers, magazines, and television channels in America: the *Wall Street Journal*, the *New York Times, Financial Times, BusinessWeek, Fortune, Forbes*, CNBC, Fox Business.

Seldom, if ever, do these media outlets present the marketing side of the story.

Sure, they talk about marketing, but only in management terms: building better products, offering a full line, quickly expanding the brand, targeting the center of the market, concentrating resources on a single brand, marketing cleverness, perpetual growth, creating customers for life, taking advantage of coupons and sales, constant innovation, utilizing multimedia, and especially the application of plain-old common sense.

All of these concepts make sense. They just don't make marketing sense. Management will never understand marketing. Why should it? Management has many other important things to worry about: production, finance, legal issues, employee recruitment, government relations.

To sell a marketing concept to management, a marketing person should keep this principle in mind: *Left-brain management will never understand right-brain marketing.*

So is the battle lost?

Not at all. But a marketing person has to sell a marketing idea to management in management terms, not in marketing terms.

A marketing person has to use analytical tools to help sell holistic concepts. A marketing person has to use facts, figures, market shares, and other data to sell intuitive ideas to a logical thinker.

Which is why this book is loaded with case histories that document what works and what doesn't work in marketing.

Don't just sell a concept, sell an analogy: "We should do what Grey Goose did. Launch a high-end brand, even though there's no market yet for a high-end product or service."

Or: "We should do what Southwest Airlines did. Launch a low-end brand, even though there's no market yet for a low-end product or service."

Or: "We should do what Apple did. Launch a second brand like the iPod."

Marketing people should think conceptually, but present their conceptual ideas to management with analogies buttressed by logical, analytical explanations.

Marketing people should sell visual ideas in verbal terms.

Talk about "hammers" instead of iconic illustrations. Talk about product benefits and features instead of positioning the brand in the mind.

(Management minds are not on the same wavelength as marketing minds.)

Most important of all, don't give up the fight.

With the weight of evidence on the marketing side of the table, let's carry the message to the management side of the table whenever we get the opportunity.

Onward, marketing soldiers.

Note on Sources

Readers will have noted our extensive use of automobile examples. Because of state vehicle registration laws and progressive publications such as *Automotive News,* a wealth of auto data is available going all the way back to 1893. No other industry comes close.

The marketing profession would be greatly enhanced if other industries gathered and shared sales data to the same extent.

Our use of ten-year profit-and-loss data is also worth mentioning. Any company can shift numbers from one year to the next, but you can't hide your financial health over a decade's time. Sooner or later, a company runs out of financial tricks.

The stock prices and market capitalization data used in the text were calculated on November 12, 2008.

Index